Arab Political Humour

Arab Political Humour
Khalid Kishtainy

Quartet Books
London New York Melbourne

First published by Quartet Books Limited 1985
A member of the Namara Group
27/29 Goodge Street, London W1P 1FD

Copyright © 1985 by Khalid Kishtainy

British Library Cataloguing in Publication Data

Kishtainy, Khalid
  Arab political humour
  1. Arabic wit and humor — History and criticism
  2. Near East in literature   3. Arab countries in literature
  I. Title
  892'.77'009358   PJ7578

ISBN 0-7043-2485-7

Phototypeset by AKM Associates (UK) Ltd,
Ajmal House, Hayes Road, Southall, Greater London
Printed and bound in Great Britain
by Mackays of Chatham Ltd, Kent

Contents

Preface

Writing on the political humour of the Arab World, past and present, is a hazardous undertaking which I was resolved to risk, much against the advice of many friends. Some felt a shudder at the thought of tackling the sense of humour of the Prophet Muhammad and the holy imams of Islam, and counselled that the subject matter should be confined to modern times. Others, however, felt a similar shudder at the thought of telling and discussing the political jokes about contemporary leaders of the modern Arab World and advised me to confine myself to the days of the Prophet and the early imams. After all, these are men of God and are guided by his spirit of indulgence and forgiveness. They are, furthermore, dead and buried and have no recourse to the revenge squads despatched from the Middle East to the four corners of the world. Yet, a full picture of Arab political humour truly reflecting the psychology, thought and politics of the Arab peoples cannot be adequately drawn without covering the entire span of Arab history, at least from the rise of Islam.

Recalling that a critic is a failed artist, I can draw from my personal experience and add that a historian of political humour may be only an intimidated humorist. But having accepted, at least, the challenge of the present book, there remained the other, no less daunting, challenge of finding the material. Political humour is a relatively recent subject of study, little acknowledged by the Arabs. To secure sufficient material for his assessment and analysis, the researcher has therefore to sift through the heavy bulk of jokes, anecdotes, fables and satirical poems scattered in many books and collections.

Jokes and jibes were never recorded at the time of telling, the eventual narrator having only his memory to rely upon, and the material became subject to the usual transformations of oral literature as it passed by word of mouth. Narrators, each according to his ability, time and place, and free from the constraints of poetry's rhymes and meter, took ample liberty in adapting or improving on the reported material. This had applied to Ash'ab as it did to Shakespeare and Brecht. Some of them found it more effective to ascribe the funny story to famous comics, which may explain how funny characters like Juha and Abu Nuwas attracted such bulky and sometimes contradictory and implausible legacies. It was found that by attributing a funny story to a famous funny man rather than to its authentic originator, more laughter could be drawn from the listener or reader by association or suggestion. All this makes it extremely hard, or rather impossible, to trace each story to its true origin and authenticate the exact words exchanged in the repartee. This situation is even more noticeable in the world of politics where the same joke is often borrowed by one nation from another, or adapted from one situation to another. It is, therefore, futile to treat as historical fact any attributed words or acts without some reliable documentation to this or that Arab leader in this book. Curiously enough, many of the people whom I have contacted to verify a story or solicit some contribution asked to be excused as soon as they heard of my project.

Some of the jokes may indeed have been of Western origin. What the reader should look for is the significance of their selection, importation and application. It is noticeable, for example, that the Arabs imported many of their jokes in the thirties and forties from western Europe whereas eastern Europe became the source in the seventies and eighties, signifying not only the fruition of the new contact with the socialist countries but also disenchantment with socialism. The kind of joke related by any man is a good indicator of his character, mood and circumstance – a fact which is as valid when applied to the nation as a whole. It is a general picture this book tries to depict rather than the detailed idiosyncrasies of any political leader.

Having read through many of the contemporary Arabic collections and biographies connected with the subject of humour, I could not help the feeling that they were often written by some of the dullest authors. The task of translation became one of rewriting, which has always been the approach of all humour writers in history. No apology is called for in this respect.

Whatever amount of reading and research one may undertake, a book on this subject is bound to evolve from the personal experience and knowledge of its author. Not having stayed long enough in many parts of the Arab World, my collection and selection of jokes and anecdotes are restricted to the countries which I happen to know well. Over-indulgence in the humour of

Egypt and the Fertile Crescent does not mean that other Arab countries, especially those of the Maghreb, are lacking in this field or deprived of any sense of humour. Apology here is more than due for this and any other unfortunate, but unavoidable omission.

NATIONALISTE.

'The Amnesty of the Khedive', Yaqub Sannu', *Abu Naddara* 1881

Introduction
The Function of Political Humour

> Why did nature endow only man with laughter? The
> answer is very simple. No other animal was burdened with
> so many woes as man.
>
> Ahmad Amin

Political humour is an advanced stage of humour and a relatively
recent development in man's history. But then, humour itself is a
late development, both on individual and collective levels. A child
is born with a cry and goes on crying for the flimsiest reasons, but its
parents have to wait for many weeks before they see its first smile.
Many ancient societies had bequeathed various epics, lamentations
and songs but not until we reach the fifth century B.C. do we hear of
anything resembling the comic. According to Aristotle, the
Megarians had claimed comedy for themselves in the days of
democracy. This is not simply due to articulation and sophistication,
but also to the need for sufficient contradictions in society to feed
the sense of humour. Henri Bergson, one of the prominent analysts
of laughter, traced many of the causes of laughter to rigidity and
inertia. To him, life is supple, the comic is rigid and repetitive, and
when life and nature are 'mechanically tampered with, we possess a
thoroughly comic theme'. Dealing with the frequent linguistic jokes
(so abundant in Arabic), he applied the same criterion, 'Pedantry . . .
at the bottom is nothing else than art pretending to outdo nature'.[1]
    In a primitive society, life is still supple, the norms are fresh and
language is free. It is when life becomes complex and society full of
contradictions and contrasts that certain things emerge as out of
place, incongruous, distorted and consequently funny. Most modern
theoreticians on the subject of laughter dwell on the idea of
contradiction in one form or another as the basis of the comic. They
see that jokes imply contrast of ideas and union of contradictions, or
as Theodor Vischer put it, 'The joker likes best to wed couples
whose union their relatives frown upon.' In his essay, 'Physiology of

laughter', Herbert Spencer attributes laughter to an accumulation of nervous energy which begets muscular motion, but when consciousness is transferred from great things to small, the liberated nerve-force – no longer required – spends itself in the muscular movement of laughter. An example of this may be found in the case of a crowd watching a dictator stumbling over a step just when he was about to harangue them with another speech. The association of laughter with energy and its function as an outlet for a disposable unwanted surplus is illustrated by Bergson in observing as symptoms of laughter many physiological actions including the increased secretion of the adrenal glands, increased sugar in the blood, acceleration of heart rate, altered breathing, inhibition of the digestive activities, changes in electric skin resistance, sweating, goose-pimples, dilation of the pupils, muscle tension and tremor. (Someone had the thought of counting fifteen facial muscles as involved in a single laugh.)

Arthur Koestler developed the theory of the bisociation which arises and produces a comic effect when there is an idea or event with two incompatible matrices.[2] He gives as one example a certain *marquis* of Louis XIV who found his wife in the arms of the bishop. The *marquis* went to the window and started to bless the people outside. 'What are you doing?' asked the wife. 'Monseigneur is performing my function. So I am performing his,' said the husband. Two opposing matrices. In another example, he cites the epigram, 'A sadist is a person who is kind to a masochist.' Kindness here is bisociated with two different meanings: first the sadist does kindness to the masochist by torturing him; secondly he is torturing the masochist by being kind to him. To appreciate the comic, Koestler went on, one must pass the animal stage and acquire a relative sense of security and reason. The fact of the contradiction was also seized by Schopenhauer when he referred to laughter as a sudden perception of incongruity between a concept and real objects. This is a notion echoed by the modern Arab thinker, Abbas Mahmud al-Aqqad: 'Laughter is therefore a sudden and fast comparison between the state in front of you and the state which you imagine, the state in being and the state required . . . This fast and intelligent comparison is only possible for a mind capable of conjuring up the ideal and genuine forms of things and their correct and desirable facets.'[3] That is why cartoonists, impersonators of politicians and petty dictators emulating Hitler or Napoleon make us laugh.

Viewed from this angle, humour is the natural medium for

representing politics in an artistic and intellectual form. It gives reason, according to Koestler, precedence over emotions and demands sufficient detachmant and self-criticism. The superiority of laughter, which often involved derision, was indeed grasped not only by Koestler but also by Bergson and, much earlier, by Hobbes and Swift.

The clash between the concept and reality, the natural and the incongruous, or between one matrice and another is associated with the idea of surprise or astonishment, which is often mentioned by doctors and philosophers. Arab jesters, like Abu al-Ibar, often applied 'inversion' as a practical application of surprise, and Arab theoreticians drew attention to it as far back as the tenth century. Abu Hayyan al-Tawhidi wrote of laughter as a power between reason and animality performing its function when the soul reaches a state of astonishment which compels it to search for the causes of the things that take place. On the other hand, it is also connected with the power of the animal. This power moves in different directions producing correspondingly different moods in the person like anger, joy, indifference, etc. 'But if it is pulled once in an inward direction, and then again in an outward direction, it generates various states. One of them is laughter. It is generated when the two powers are pulled in different directions in search of the reason.' In *Bustan al-Atibba*, Ibn al-Mutran, the twelfth-century doctor, also refers to astonishment as the source of laughter, when the soul is overwhelmed with astonishment and finds speech inadequate to express itself. 'Thus those who are unable to express the astonishment they feel are seen to associate speech with laughter in order to supplement the expression . . .'[4] Modern thinkers like Lipps and Heymans also endorsed the notion of 'bewilderment and illumination' as the fountain source of laughter.

Another important point in humour relevant to political life is its communal character. We all enjoy a comic film more in the cinema than at home on television and laugh louder when a joke is told by a speaker to a large audience than by a friend over a cup of tea, or when we read it in a book. Unlike weeping, which is personal and private, laughing is exhibitionist and public. 'Our laughter is always the laughter of the group,' said Bergson, who likened the community of the laughing with that of freemasonry, a description whose validity may be demonstrated under the shadow of political oppression when the subjects circulate among themselves stealthily jokes and innuendoes loaded with symbolism and ritualism. The electric effect of a good joke or jibe delivered in a meeting is something which most politicians appreciate and try to utilize.

Most philosophers pointed to the corrective effect of laughter, and until modern times, applied the Aristotelian theory on the subject. It was assumed that man's moods were subject to the balance or imbalance of the four body fluids, or humours: blood, phlegm, choler (yellow bile) and melancholy (black bile). Any excess of one at the expense of the others produced an abnormality which could be corrected by projecting it to the subject concerned through the medium of satire and laughter. Comedy, according to Aristotle, was based on the ridiculous, which is either a mistake or a deformity. It was the representation of inferior people and 'consists in some blunder or ugliness that does not cause a disaster, an obvious example being the comic mask which is ugly and distorted but not painful'.[5] The Greek teachings were taken over by the Arabs who also upheld the physiological origin of laughter and the theory of the four humours. Ibn al-Mutran divined that good-quality blood gives joy and joy gives laughter. Like other Arab doctors, he placed humour in a favourable light and commended its beneficial use. Medieval thinkers and comic writers followed suit and expanded on the remedial character of laughter and humour.

Although much of that highly optimistic view of laughter as a corrective was eroded, the belief in its useful function has persisted. In his classic study, Bergson followed up his idea of rigidity by stating that comedy is its sure treatment. The subject is unaware of his defects, and the more unaware he is the more comic he becomes. This is the opposite of the dramatic, but once the comic realizes these laughable defects, he begins to correct them. Hence comedy corrects men's manners.[6]

Jokes represent a revolt against authority and a liberation from its pressure, which explains their frequent use against the high and mighty. 'A joke will allow us to exploit something ridiculous in our enemy, which we could not on account of obstacles in the way, bring forward openly or consciously; . . . the joke will evade restrictions and open sources of pleasure that have become inaccessible. It will further bribe the bearer with its yield of pleasure into taking sides with us . . .'[7] Freud's last sentence is a reformulation of Aristotle's idea that 'comic expressions, though they go so far as to be incredible, yet sound convincing because they are laughable'.

Many politicians and political writers have awakened to this fact and have warned against the stealthy onslaught of political jokes. Humour as a 'weapon in battle' has become a slogan in many lands including the Arab World, where many journals and newspapers have been clamouring for a revival of this weapon, long put under lock and key by the present rulers.

Yet, there seems to be an overstatement of the case of humour as a remedy. In fact, the opposite may be true, and we may well find that joking about things is only a form of escapism. We have seen how modern analysts of humour attribute laughter to a peaceful release of energy mobilized for something more serious. A witty speaker can easily disarm an angry opposition by entertaining them with his wit and jokes, and the Arabs have said that an eloquent thief need not have his hand chopped off. Politicians know this and tend to resort to it whenever they find themselves short of positive rational answers. Hence its frequent use by such great parliamentarians as Disraeli, Lloyd George, Churchill and Bevan. Laughter is truly attached to reason and to a higher level of intellect, but such is the magic of humour that the power of reasoning can be guided into any direction. Escapism is the obvious explanation for the most universal type of jokes, the jokes about mothers-in-law and matrimony. Here a joke is the only bloodless escape from an inescapable situation. If more men learn to joke, perhaps there will be less women beaten up. The analogy to that is the jokes about minorities and neighbouring nations. The Greeks were the first to register their mockery of foreigners by laughing at their barbarous speaking: *bar ... bar ... bar ... bar*. But they could not do without trading with them, employing them and living with them.

In that sense, and as Freud put it, humour is quite useful in diverting aggressive or lustful tendencies. But as a positive weapon in the battle against oppression, its use is of doubtful efficacy. People joke about their oppressors, not to overthrow them but to endure them, and the more durable and formidable the regime may be, the more resort is made to humour. Richter's maxim: 'Freedom produces jokes and jokes produce freedom', must therefore be taken with a good pinch of salt. We have often heard of dramatic and musical performances ending with demonstrations and clashes, but I still have to hear of a comic performance turned to anger or action. Of course, comedy does enlighten the people and focus their attention on the problem, but it very rarely discovers for them anything which they did not know already. It was plays like *Cathy Come Home* and *Look Back in Anger* which spotlighted the plight of the homeless and the frustration of the young, and not the television comedians or Vicky's cartoons. In fact, jokes presuppose an advanced awareness of the problem in the mind of the listener, or else they fall flat. Therefore, rulers may be ill-advised in allowing their sensitivity to get the upper hand and cause them to suppress what may be actually useful to them.

In the contemporary world of the Arabs, we can find practically all the reasons which make humour relevant to politics. There is the great gap between the earlier promises and hopes, the sense of past glory, the rich resources, the strategic position and the human potential on the one hand, and the political chaos, tyranny, dismemberment, fratricide and successive failures and defeats on the other. It is a perfect contrast between the conception and reality. What is more, the Arabs seem to find themselves in an inescapable situation. So much has been invested in the feud with Isreal, yet they find themselves less and less capable of doing anything about it. The promises of justice and welfare are frustrated by the centuries of corruption and nepotism, and aspiration towards democracy and freedom is blocked by an even longer history of despotic rule. Deprived of the channels for free discussion, criticism and self-expression, the citizen is left with nothing but escapism. The skilled and qualified do it physically by emigration, the religious by resorting to fundamentalism, the dissipated by indulging in sex, drugs and drink, the rational and witty by laughing – and the poor by crying.

'The Devil carrying Egypt's enemies into hell',
Yaqub Sannu', *Abu Naddara* 1896

1 The *Zarif* and His Art

> Do not out of piety or piosity raise your eyebrow and look
> askance at the mention of the [sexual] organs for there is no
> sin in that. The sin is to defame honour, tell lies and give
> false witness.
>
> Ibn Qutayba

In the long controversy which raged during the Golden Age of the
Arab Empire (8th–10th century A.D.) between the Arabs and the
Shu'ubids (non-Arab subjects) the spokesmen of Arabism defended
the superiority of the Arab mind by referring to Arabic literature.[1]
One of such spokesmen was al-Jahiz, who contrasted the cultural
contributions of the Arabs with those of the Shu'ubids by asserting
in his *Al-Bayan wa al-Tabiyn* (Rhetoric and Elucidation) that the
Arabs are people of the tongue – meaning literature and language.
This truism was generally accepted and Arabic literature has
become one of the treasures of human creativeness. Yet, despite a
rich and varied literature, the Arabs are not so readily associated in
the minds of Westerners with humour or wit, which usually makes
up a sizeable chunk of any nation's literature and oral folklore.
Indeed, one can even perceive that the opposite, i.e. temper, ill-
humour, melancholy, gloom, stern looks, etc., is the generally
accepted picture associated with the Arab character.

As desert nomads ever on the move, the natives of the Arabian
peninsula could not develop any art which presupposed a settled life
– like architecture, sculpture, painting and drama. The only art form
which the nomad could afford was the one which required the least
carriage, weight and space. He found that within the confined space
of his brain he could pack thousands of verses and millions of words
which could then be unpacked at a moment's notice to give instant
enjoyment. Against the empty expanses of sand dunes, he developed
this pleasure-giving asset to a magic abstract world of words in
which language became the end and not the means. It is obvious
that in the lonely desert, what the traveller longs for is the human

voice, regardless of its content. Next to nomadic wandering after pasture, commerce was practically the only other occupation which the natives of Arabia pursued. In his *Foundations of Christianity*, K. Kantsky observed that unlike farmers and craftsmen who produce tangible things and consequently express themselves in concrete forms, traders deal with money – that most abstract form of man's belongings – and goods, which are merely numbered items for them. They can be boxes or parcels whose contents they may not even see. Therefore, everything conspired to make the mental and artistic preoccupation of the Arabs utterly abstract. Algebra, music, geometric art, symmetrical decoration, austere monotheism, rhythmical poetry, geometrical rhymes, linguistic disputations and intricate figures of speech became the intellectual pleasures of the Arabs.

Whereas the branches of algebra, mathematics, geometry and decorative arts thrilled and enriched mankind, the verbal branches made very little impression on the non-Arabic-speaking public. No example in evidence of this is better than the Qur'an. To the Arabs this holy book is considered, solely on its artistic and literary merits, as Muhammad's main, if not only miracle. The words of the Qur'an are the words of God himself and no human being can come anywhere near to their divine excellence. Yet, to most Europeans, the Holy Qur'an, translated into their own languages, is one of the most tedious, repetitive and incomprehensible books.

Arabic more or less lost its function to the literate as a means of expression and came to be moulded and shaped just like a piece of wonderful clay in the hands of a sculptor. For the purpose of our enquiry, this has meant that the bulk of Arabic literary and verbal genius depended on the beauty and force of the words, their sounds, their arrangement, their rhythm and their association. The verbal character presents the translator with an impossible task and the foreign recipient with a hopeless undertaking. 'Should they translate the wisdom of the Arabs,' wrote al-Jahiz in his *Book of Animals*, 'that miracle which is the meter would disappear and they would find nothing in it which has not been already said by the foreigners in their books.' This applies to divinity just as it applies to obscenity and to the verses of the lyrical poet as to the repartee of the wit.

The intricate and delicate configuration of the characters of the Arabic alphabet together with the customary omission of the vowels helped to create endless jibes and jokes which are completely confined to the Arabic reader. You only need a tiny dot, for example, to turn the letter R into Z. With the playful or accidental addition of such a dot the word *rabbi* (my God) can be turned into *zubbi* (my penis)! The door was thus opened for one satirical wit to make his dutiful comment and correct an otherwise unwarranted statement. Some humble person married a rich widow with whose money he built himself an imposing mansion which he piously adorned with the legend, carefully engraved over the door, 'Such are the blessings of my God' (*Hada min fadl rabbi*). The local wit hastened under cover of darkness to put matters right by adding the missing dot to change the hallowed phrase into 'Such are the blessings of my penis'.

The Arabs revel in this kind of linguistic humour. Arabic grammar, the cherished love of all literate Arabs, constantly requires maddening changes in the vowels of words according to their gender, tense, condition and position in the sentence. The puzzling complexity is further compounded by the usual refusal to put down the vowel signs. The murderer becomes the murdered, and 'God curses the infidels' becomes 'God curses his prophets'. The preposition 'until' (*hatta*) is a typical grammatical enigma in Arabic. Lying on his death bed, a grammarian was heard to utter his last words, 'O "until", I die with thee in my mind.' The celebrated modern thinker, Taha Hussein, commented on the subject and said that while other peoples read in order to educate themselves, the Arabs educate themselves in order to read. But the inevitable confusion, mistakes, misreading and misunderstanding coming out of such a linguistic fairyland, proved to be a fertile ground for yet another species of humour.

Almost every Arabic proper noun conveys a definite meaning like *hussein* (pretty), *sadiq* (truthful), *jamil* (beautiful), *khalid* (immortal), *sa'id* (happy), *muhammed* (blessed), *salim* (safe), etc. This has enabled everybody to play on their opponents' names and produce ready-made satirical jibes. The former Iraqi President, Abd al-Salam (Servant of Peace) was thus called and with good effect, Servant of War and Enemy of Peace by al-Jawahiri in one of his memorable caustic poems. During the bitter quarrel between Tunisia and Egypt in the fifties, a Cairo Radio comedian played on Habib Bourguiba's name, which meant 'Habib the Neck', and asked his fellow comedian: 'Why did they call the President of Tunisia "Bourguiba"?'

'Because he has a long neck.'

'No.'

'Because he has a short neck.'

'No.'

'Because he has a fat neck.'

'No.'

'Then why, for God's sake, tell me.'

'Because the imperialists are leading him by the neck.'

Bourguiba answered in kind and played on the presumptuous and outdated official name of Egypt, 'The United Arab Republic', and paused in one of his speeches to ask 'united with whom?'.

The sarcastic misuse of names has not been always as polite or free from resort to the equivalent of the English four-letter words. In the fierce and often bloody strife between the Ba'th Party and the Nasserists and Communists, the opponents of the Ba'th played on the strange name of the founder and leader of the Ba'th Party, Michel Aflaq. One of the latest exercises in this respect was the discovery in Al-Muhit lexicon that Aflaq meant in archaic Arabic 'wide and loose vagina and stupid, sluttish woman'.

The old nomadic dislike of all crafts and dislike of all craftsmen provided another source of satire. To the Arabs, a true Arab gentleman is one who gets his money without ever working for it. You may well find pure Arabs giving themselves names like Stone, Hill, Sword and Lion, but never Smith, Tailor, Mason, Silverman or Carpenter. The use of such names among the mongrel townspeople and altogether the involvement in such crafts, or indeed any work whatsoever, opened the way for easy satire and mockery. The former Iraqi Prime Minister, Abd al-Rahman al-Bazzaz was repeatedly mocked in his electioneering campaigns for being a bazzaz (cloth dealer). As a professor at the Faculty of Law, Dr Bazzaz had to weather the secondary jibe of being actually a teacher, something which is associated in the minds of his countrymen with child-ishness and immaturity and which had inspired al-Jahiz and many other authors to write many an amusing anecdote on the subject, as will be mentioned. The cruel Iraqis also discovered that Nasser was the son of a postman, and went on in their 1958 feud with Cairo to torment the Egyptian leadership, or so they thought, by repeatedly playing over the radio Asmahan's song about her postman 'El-Postajia Ishtaku' (The Postmen are Complaining).

Ever since the rise of Islam, the Qur'an has been the main book of learning in the Arab World, and many Muslims know by heart the entire book, or at least many chapters of it. Quotations from the holy book and the early great poems have occupied a central place in the life and literature of the Arabs, which paved the way for another type of humour based on the hyperbolic use of religious and classical texts. The comic misapplication of the holy scripture known to medieval Europe and many other parts of the world has been even more frequent in the Arab World in view of this mass popularity and accessibility of the Qur'an. All the wealth of witty

remarks and amusing anecdotes woven around the playful misapplication and misquotation of the poets and the Qur'an is totally lost
on the aliens who are hardly at home with the nuances and
implications of the emotive verses.

Above all, we are dealing here with the literature and humour of a
people separated from the contemporary world of Europe and
America by some ten centuries and a few thousand miles. With its
reliance on topicality and existing circumstances and personalities,
comedy is the most transient of the muses. The jokes which were
born out of the long feuds between the various sects and clans
require pages of explanations to make them intelligible to most
contemporary readers. This difficulty extends from the subject
matter to the style, as the western concepts of humour, wit, irony,
comedy, parody, etc. do not exactly fit into the Arabian concepts of
fukaha, mizah, hazal, zarf, etc. There is no consensus on what the
Western terms actually embrace and I am not going to try and find
definitions for the Arabic terms, but the most serious shortcoming
on the Arab side is the omission of comedy. The stage is the best
ground for the development and interplay of the comic and
humorous motifs and, as Bergson remarked, 'A witty nation is, of
necessity, a nation enamoured of the theatre'. In his lecture on *The
Idea of Comedy*, George Meredith drew attention to the important
role of women in comedy which made the comic muse one of the
best friends of the gentle sex, and went on to relate how an Arab
interlocuter was incensed by the suggestion that the Arabs might
benefit from emancipating their womenfolk. 'Eastward you have
total silence of comedy,' Meredith commented, 'among a people
intensely susceptible to laughter, as the *Arabian Nights* will testify.
Where the veil is over women's faces, you cannot have society
without which the senses are barbarous and the comic spirit is
driven to the gutters of grossness to slake its thirst. Arabs in this
respect are worse than Italians – much worse than Germans; just in
the degree that their system of treating women is worse . . .

'There has been fun in Baghdad. But there never will be
civilization where comedy is not possible; and that comes of some
degree of social equality of the sexes.'[2]

Meredith was no expert in Arabic literature or history and
altogether missed the point that the Arabs had no theatre. The other
point which he missed was that the medieval despotism of the East
did not apply to women only but to the bulk of society. The
development of drama is closely related to the development of
democracy with its acquiescence in plurality, freedom of discussion

and repartee, cognizance of other points of view and collective teamwork. That is why the theatre prospered in Greece, western Europe and the Anglo-Saxon world. The extreme individualism of the Arabs, the austere nomadic life of the desert and the despotism of the East militated against the establishment of the theatre, with detrimental consequences on the comic branches of art. T.E. Lawrence described in his *Revolt in the Desert* how the warriors of the Howeitat were thrilled by the new art form of parody, which they witnessed for the first time in their lives, as he went on mimicking their leader. The absence of experience in theatrical comedy manifests its negative effects in the untidy way in which Arab authors have often told their jokes and in their unawareness of such stylistic ingredients as brevity, crispness, timing and finishing, which comedians normally acquire from years of work on the stage.

Infused with an inflated sense of personal pride, belligerence and intolerance associated with the intense struggle for survival and constant tribal warfare, the poet evolved that great chapter of Arabic literature, the *hijá* (satire), a merciless onslaught on the enemy, which sometimes led to murder, as in the case of al-Mutanabbi, the leading Arab poet, who mocked Dhabba al-Atbi in these words:

People did no justice to Dhabba
Or his breasts-sagging dwarf of a mother.
They flung aside his father's head,
And mounted his mother by force.
The dead reaped no glory
And the ravished fulfilled no desire.
Is it such a disgrace
That your mother is a whore?
Or that a dog is aggrieved
That he is a bitch's son?
She suffered no harm when she was topped,
He who topped her harmed his loins.

A few years later, Dhabba's uncle lay in wait for the poet as he journeyed from Baghdad and murdered him. *Il comedia il finito*. This ungracious method of attacking the opponent by slandering his womenfolk continued in popularity and crept into the political arena in modern times, as will be demonstrated.

Less vulgar and more amusing, however, is al-Baha' Zuhair's (d. 1258) lampoon about a bearded fellow:

A buffoon with a beard,
Spread out and large
I search for his face in it,
Yet, I could find it not.
I know him fully well,
But incognito he has become.
A bull of a wondrous shape
With a round about beard.
Had that bull been a calf,
The Israelites would have worshipped it.
Curse it of a beard!
Monstrous and disgusting!
How many hamlets the ants did build
And cemeteries around its edge.
One tenth of its tenth
Would be sufficient for ten.
The pig envies that beard
As he sees it spread
And wishes if only he could possess
Just one of its hairs.

So virulent had satire become that the Caliph Omar had to pay the famous satirist al-Hutay'ah (d. 678) three thousand dirhams to buy from him the honour of the Muslims. Running short of targets, he satirized his mother, his wife and finally himself:

My lips are longing to say something evil
Yet I know not about whom I can say it.

Al-Hutay'ah then wandered away until he came to a well where he saw the reflection of his face in the water. At last he had found a target.

I see a face disfigured by Allah.
Curse that face and curse its carrier.

Against this background of verbal fencing, the Arab equivalent of the British sport, one must try to view the virulence of inter-Arab verbal warfare and the ease and loving kisses with which it invariably ends, often sealed and concluded with a new joint pledge for unity and the setting up of a new council for unification. Satire and sarcasm suited the individualist temperament and factional

strife, but the Arab love for entertainment, especially oral entertainment, helped to overcome the obstacles just discussed and left
us with a rich heritage worthy of transmission to any generation and
climate. 'Men are in prison unless they indulge in humour,' said an
old Arabic proverb. Historians cite numerous examples of early
Arab humour involving even the Prophet Muhammad himself, who
was probably the only prophet credited with instances of jest and
court jesters. This is to be expected from a man endowed with a fine
poetic appreciation. 'Mind the crockery!' was one of his utterances to
the men who were helping the women to their horses. In another
instance, he asked a man who was giving evidence of his wife's
adultery, 'Have you seen the stick in the *kohl* pot?' To be humorous
is to be free of anger and there is no record of the Prophet ever losing
his temper, despite all the provocations and aggravations he had to
endure. Blessed with a rare receptivity, tolerance, indulgence and
broad mind, he joked with his companions, laughed at their antics
and recommended humour to the faithful. 'From hour to hour,
refresh your hearts for if they tire, they will lose their insight,' he
advised. In another saying he struck at the relationship between
humour and philosophy: 'I joke and say nothing but the truth.'

His council seems to have been full of innocent mirth and
practical jokes. Nuwairi related that the Prophet once said to a
woman from the Partisans, 'Hurry to your husband! He has some
white in his eyes.' The woman rushed home in panic only to be told
by her husband, 'Why, I do have harmless white in my eyes.'[3] On
meeting an old woman one day, he told her that old women would
not enter paradise. The woman was thus deeply upset – then
Muhammad hastened to remind her of the Qur'anic verse that all
women would revert to their youth in paradise. In another instance,
the Prophet himself became the subject of a practical joke, when
Nu'ayman al-Mazih, the equivalent of the European court jester, saw
a Bedouin selling a jar of honey which he bought from him and
instructed him to deliver to Muhammad. The Prophet was pleased
and divided the jar among his companions. That done, the Bedouin
asked for his money. It was cash on delivery. 'Oh, this is one of
Nu'ayman's pranks!' said the Prophet. Soon, Nu'ayman appeared and
asked for his share. 'Wherefore?' he was asked. 'I wanted your
blessing, Messenger of God, but had nothing to pay for it,' he
answered. Ibn Qutaiba relates how the Prophet went on laughing for
a whole year as the result of another prank in which Nu'ayman sold
a free man to a Bedouin. Historians often depict Muhammad as
laughing heartily in many situations.

More than one scholar dwelt on the theme of humour in the Qur'an wherein the function of laughter is mentioned in many places as one of God's blessings, miracles and signs of fulfilment as well as an expression of ridicule. In the ninth century, al-Jahiz dealt with the subject and drew attention in his Introduction to *Kitab al-Bukhala* (The Book of Misers) to God's approval of laughter by citing the Qur'anic verse: 'It was He who caused laughter and caused weeping and it was He who brought death and gave life.' In more recent times, Abbas Mahmud al-Aqqad, the modern Egyptian writer, listed the instances in which the Qur'an mentioned laughter with approbation and quoted the following verse as a comic narrative verging on the cariacature: 'When they reached the ants' valley, an ant said, "O, ants, get into your homes or else Solomon and his soldiers may crush you unaware!" Then Solomon smiled laughingly at its words and said, "O, God allow me to thank you for your blessings . . .".'[4]

The spirit of humour embraced many of Muhammad's close companions among whom Uthman, the second caliph, was an outstanding example. He was reported to have been blessed by the Prophet in a singular manner when he said, 'Uthman will enter paradise laughing, because he made me laugh.' How he made him laugh may be guessed from the story when the Prophet saw him eating dates while one of his eyes was afflicted with ophthalmia. 'What! Eating dates when your eye is afflicted?' Uthman answered: 'I am eating from the other side.'

However, Uthman certainly laughed on the other side of his face when he himself became the target of a painful joke. Nu'ayman led a blind man inside the mosque and told him, 'There! You can urinate here.' When the man was shouted at and hustled out, he swore to take revenge on his deceiver. Nu'ayman then reappeared. 'Do you want to take your revenge on that Nu'ayman? Come!' He led him to where the caliph was praying and the blind man fell on him with his stick! Soon after the death of Muhammad, he became the first Muslim ruler to include in his entourage a professional court jester, the clownish Ash'ab the Greedy.

The love of humour and jest is expressed in many forms. It is noteworthy, for example, that many of the Arabic nouns for jokes and humour suggest food and eating. *Fukaha* (humour) is a derivative of *Fakiha* (fruit), *mulha* (anecdote) is a derivative of *milh* (salt), *nadira* (droll story) is a derivative of *nadir* (rare), *nukta* (joke) is a derivative associated with *nukat* (ripened dates), *hazal* (jest) is a noun meaning both jesting and leanness and *zarf* (wit) is the vessel bringing you food presents. Such an association is by no means accidental or devoid of significance, for in the barren deserts and mountains of the Arabian Peninsula the search for food and water is the most pressing preoccupation of the inhabitants. The act of devouring and feasting inspired entire worlds of concepts, pleasures and traditions extending from the vision of paradise with its flowing rivers and lush fruits to the more immediate custom of hospitality. The eternal quest for food and sustenance and outright begging for meals, charity and reward constituted a major chapter in Arabic poetry and literature.

Even in our own present time, poets compose eulogies or satires about kings and heads of state in expectation of gifts and gains. The heads of state, on the other hand, deem it expedient to influence the international press and governments of the great powers by giving the visiting correspondent or diplomat a jolly good meal. Many cynical remarks were made on the Palestinian leaders' habit of throwing lavish banquets for foreign pressmen and academics in attempts to focus their attention on the plight and starvation of the Palestinians.

On the other hand, the devices and tricks to eke out a living, secure a free meal and devour as much as possible – or impossible – at a banquet, inspired hundreds of jokes and witty anecdotes. This theme was given its artistic footing by Uthman's jester, Ash'ab the Greedy (d.771), who was the first professional wit and comedian in Arab history. He was born during the lifetime of Muhammad to an infamous woman at Medina, where he was trained as an entertainer. With blue eyes, dark skin and a peculiar face amenable to freakish distortions and grimaces, he could not fail to amuse his clients with his singing, dancing and tomfoolery. Franz Rosenthal, who made an extensive study of this comedian and his art, concluded that despite the existence of similar jokes in Greek literature, Ash'ab's anecdotes remained original and typical.[5] Notwithstanding that most of these anecdotes – which fill many Arabic works, especially *Kitab al-Aghani* (The Book of Songs) – were woven around his personality at a later age and in the flourishing city of Baghdad, they expressed a native life-style based on endemic poverty, scarcity and dependence. The following are typical samples of the Ash'ab anecdotes.

– He saw some people eating fish and hastened to join them: 'I have great animosity and wrath against fish because my father was eaten by them when he drowned at sea.' Fearing that he would pick up the biggest, they threw a small one to him. 'There you are. Avenge the death of your father.' He put the fish to his ear and said, 'Do you know, this one has just said that he was not born when my father died. "Look to the big ones there," it said. "They were around at that time and ate your father." ' Ash'ab then snatched the biggest fish from the tray.

– Ash'ab was asked whether he had ever seen anyone greedier than himself. He answered, 'Yes. A dog which followed me for four miles after seeing me chewing gum.'

– 'I had a dream,' he said 'half of which came true, but the other half did not.' He was then asked about it and he replied: 'I dreamt that I was carrying a load of money and because of its heavy weight I soiled my clothes. When I woke up I found that my clothes were soiled all right, but there was no money.'

– 'What are you eating?' he asked some companions of the Prophet, who snapped back at him, 'Poisonous fish!' Ash'ab then dived with his hand into the tray of food saying, 'Life after the death of the Prophet's companions is not worth living.'

– Having found a dinar in the street, he was told that he should advertise the fact in accordance with Islamic law. Ash'ab then bought a blanket with the dinar and toured the town asking whether anyone had a claim on it. He then asked his friends, 'Do you think the dinar was sufficiently advertised?'

– In answer to a question about the extent of his greed, he said, 'I have never seen two people in a discussion without hoping that they might be discussing giving me something.'

Like all good clowns, Ash'ab had that trace of bitter sadness about his jokes. 'They ask you for stories fit for kings and reward you with the gifts of slaves.' He was conscious of his peculiar appearance. 'How awful!' someone said to him. 'Your father had a respectable beard and you have this flimsy one. Whom are you taking after?'

Ash'ab replied, 'After my mother.' The question may well have stung the greedy jester because he could well have been illegitimate. He hated his mother as may be deduced from the following Freudian anecdote related by al-Mada'ini. 'Mother, I saw you in my sleep. You were covered with honey and I was covered all over with shit.'

'You accursed sinner,' she said to him, 'these are your evil deeds which God covered you with.'

'There was something else in my dream,' he continued. 'I was licking you and you were licking me.'

The hard struggle for survival amid the scarcity of food and water in barren Arabia had likewise intensified the sexual dispositions with all their drive, resistance, jealousies, obsessions and inhibitions. Rightly or wrongly, preoccupation with sex and sexual matters has become something often associated with the Arabs. This may be due to their personal conduct and interests as much as to their translated literature, well evidenced in *One Thousand and One Nights*, *The Perfumed Garden*, etc. In his analysis of sexual jokes, Freud interpreted men's interest in them as a means of seduction wherein the mention of the sexual organs is a substitute for their exposure, their exposure is a substitute for touch and touch is a prelude to coitus. When a woman opposes his joking overtures, the man calls for the support of another man, the third person, whose laughter at the joke smooths the procedure and makes the overture less objectionable to the female. All nations indulge profusely in smut and it may be quite unfair to single out the Arabs in this respect. Yet, despite the lack of comparative statistical data on the subject, I could not help the personal impression that there is an exaggerated share of smut in the written and oral literature of the Arabs. It is also interesting to note that many of the jokes in this genre came in the form of repartee between male and female – like this one. A man from Bani Lam, a tribe noted for its homosexuality, met a female and asked her, 'Tell me, my good woman, do women actually conceive from the back or the front?' The sharp-witted woman answered him, 'You wretch! If from the back, Bani Lam would have filled the world.'

Therefore, sexuality and excrementalism, which Freud links in an inextricable bond with sex, form a large section of Arab humour and Arabic jokes, coined in both verbal and conceptual forms, as well as in crude vulgarity or refined wit. Helped by the open nature of Arab society and Arab character, this indulgence found ample material and exciting fields in the crazy world of harems, concubinage, polygamy, permissible homosexuality and altogether decadent society of the late Abbasids. In the world of contemporary Arab politics, all this joke technique was shifted from its conventional usage, sublimated and reintroduced into the arena of the national struggle and partisan feuds as sheer political smut.

Tragedy speaks to the heart and comedy speaks to the intellect, hence tragedy came first and comedy thereafter in the history of drama. Most philosophers who examined the phenomenon of laughter dwelt on the question of the incongruity arising out of the contradiction between the real and objective and the conceptual and subjective. Bergson emphasized that laughter results from the mechanical tampering with nature and the clash between the rigid and the supple. In a newly born society, the natural, flexible and supple is the order of the day and, hence, man has very little to laugh about. But as time passes, society loses its flexibility and the fresh expediencies become rigid rules binding the spirit of man which every now and then liberates itself in a bout of laughter as the contradiction reaches an absurd impasse. Nowhere can this be more evident than in the phenomenon of pedantry, which incidentally fills large sections of Arabic literature and humour.

In the pre-Islamic Jahilia era, the Arabs spoke freely and the language afforded no opportunity for laughter, but by the tenth century, Arabic fell into the hands of the grammarians and linguists who set up their taboos and rigid rules and, in the ensuing clash between the real and the conceptual, opened the gate for the torrent of verbal jokes and quips. What applied to language applied to the entire social organization.

By the time the Abbasids established themselves in the ninth century, the promises and expectations were already fading and the long *jihad* (holy war) of the people was drifting to a dead end. The intuitive response of the past was giving way to intellectual cynicism and appreciation of the funny, generated and sharpened by the sophistication and culture of the new articulate society. By the time Al-Mansur acceded to the Caliphate, humour had become one of the main branches of creative writing and a series of collections of anecdotes and jokes were eventually produced by eminent authors. Practically all grammarians mentioned in the encyclopaedic *Fihrist*, wrote a tract on humour. The classic works of *Al-Iqd al-Farid* (The Unique Necklace) by Ibn Abd Rabbih, *Kitab al-Aghani* (The Book of Songs) by al-Asbahani, *Nihayat al-Arab* (The Ultimate Goal) by Nuwairi, *Al-Mahasin wa al-Maswi* (The Virtues and Defects) by Ibrahim al-Bayhaqi and *Uyun al-Akhbar* (The Fountains of Intellegence) by Ibn Qutayba contained substantial sections on jokes and humour. In the twelfth century, Ibn al-Jawzi wrote *Akhbar al-Zurafá wa al-Mutamajinin* (The Annals of Wits and Merrymen), and *Akhbar al-Hamqa wa al-Mughaffalin* (The Annals of Fools and Simpletons) in which he defended the virtue of humour. Ali al-Hakimi wrote *Al-Fukaha wa al-Du'aba* (Humour and Pleasantry) and Abu Zayd al-Ansari compiled *Kitab al-Nawadir* (The Book of Anecdotes). Al-Naysaburi produced another book with the philosophic title, *Ugala' al-Majanin* (The Sane among the Insane). An entertaining book under the title of *al-Mustatraf fi Kulli Fannin Mustazraf* (The Pleasant in Every Pleasing Art) was produced at a later date by al-Abshihi. The compilation tradition in this field continued well into our time and selections from the material were produced in German by A. Wesselski (1911) and in French by R.

Basset (1924). F. Rosenthal translated Ash'ab's jokes into English in
the book already mentioned. Many characters like Nu'ayman the
Jester, Ash'ab the Greedy, Abu Dulama, Abu Nu'as the profligate
poet, Juha, Muzabbid and Abu al-Harith Jamiz became household
names around which endless stories and witty remarks were woven
and fabricated. Historians reported that Harun al-Rashid was always
accompanied in his travels by his court jester, Abu Sadaqa.

With the growth of the cosmopolitan society of Baghdad and the
sophisticated élite of learned men, a new type of humorous and
cultured wits, known as *zurafá* appeared and attracted the attention
of both layman and scholar with their style of life and sense of
humour. Although they resembled in many respects the wits of
seventeenth-century England, they differed in their devotion to
divine matters and piety. In his book, *al-Muwasha*[6], Abu al-Tayib
al-Washa' discussed the qualities of the *zurafá* and said that *zarf*
depends on four ingredients: eloquence, rhetoric, virtue and
righteousness, but Ibn al-A'rabi insisted that *zarf* rests with the
tongue only.

Al-Washa' dealt with the life-style of the *zurafá* and described in
great detail the types of shoes, clothes, perfume and rings they wore.
On their food and table manners, he said, 'They were the first to eat
in small measures, avoid gluttony and greed, eat the middle of the
bread and the thin *bizmaward* [a kind of meat omelette]. They never
touch sinew, muscles, stomachs, spleen, lungs, sausages or meat
stew. They don't eat vegetable leaves, sip gravy or take fat . . .' He
consumed pages and pages on describing the image and manners of
the *zarif* to excessive lengths:

> To have the quality of his *zarf* complete, the *zarif* must appear in
> good apparel and smell of sweet perfume. He must show no sign
> of dirt, neither on his body nor on his clothes or pockets. His
> garment must not be torn, undone or uneven in its folds, nor
> must his trousers have any holes. He may not allow his nails to go
> long or his hair to grow wild. His armpits must not smell and his
> body should remain free from oil. The *zarif* should not have a
> running nose, soiled hand, blistering skin, spluttering mouth,
> crusted eye, or frothy lips . . .

In yet another passage al-Washa' continues to pile on the
requisites of the genuine *zurafa'*:

> Don't you see, the *zurafa'* do not beg for favours, spit on the floor,

yawn, sniff, belch or stretch their bodies. Such things are defects in a *zarif* and much disapproved of by the learned ... The *zurafa'* do not put hand on hand, clasp their fingers, stretch their legs, scratch their skin, poke their noses . . . relieve themselves or urinate in front of others ...

Against such stiff strictures, the *zurafa'* enjoyed a large measure of freedom of expression and often wrote and said things which no contemporary writer of our time could dream of writing. Indeed part of the comparative demise and oblivion into which their words have fallen is due to our puritanic inhibitions – and prohibitions – to repeat them or translate them into other languages, and this present book is no exception.

Fortified by their apparent religiousness, probity and integrity, and strengthened by their self-confidence, high breeding, education and knowledge, they were like the seventeenth-century gallants of European literature and showed similar greatness in self-criticism, irony, cynicism and satire, from which not even their own professions and hobbies were free. Nowhere was this more apparent than in their savage ridicule of the sacred cows of Arab education, grammar, language, *fiqh* and jurisprudence. A grammarian on board ship heard a sailor using foul language and asked the sailor in horror, 'Don't you know your grammar?' 'No, I don't,' replied the sailor. 'Then you have lost half of your life,' said the grammarian. Soon the ship was wrecked and the grammarian was heard amid the waves shouting for rescue. 'Don't you know how to swim?' shouted the sailor to him. 'No, I don't,' replied the man. 'Then you've lost all your life!'

Jokes about the dogmas of grammar and the pedantry of the language became a whole species of in-jokes in which Abu Alqama, himself a remarkable linguist, excelled by producing hilarious pieces based on weird archaism and verbal jumble.

The science of *balagha* (eloquence) was developed in the same period and was defined as the science of reaching your meaning with the minimum of words. I find this the biggest joke ever coined by the Arabs, and the *zurafa'* seem to have shared my feeling by ridiculing most eloquently the endless verbiage continuously churned up *ad infinitum* by the average Arab steeped in the linguistic tradition of the decadent period. Ibn Qutayba related how a Bedouin attended the prayer for rain in which the linguist, Abu Maknun, went on to excessive lengths in his most eloquent appeal to the Almighty. The Bedouin gathered his things hastily and rushed out: 'O, you successor of Noah, by the God of Qa'ba, this is going to be the Deluge itself. Let me hurry to a mountain and save my life.'

In his short story of the *Maqama al-Mudhiriya*, Badi' al-Zaman al-Hamathani relates how his hero, Abu al-Fath was invited by a linguist for a meal of *mudhiriya* (meat cooked in yoghurt). The hungry Abu al-Fath had to listen to endless descriptive passages about the meal, the woman who cooked it, the place where it was cooked, the door of the house – until he could bear it no longer and ran out of the house crazily, collided with a passer-by, slashed his head and ended up in prison.

Most of such episodes conform to the Bergsonian notion of pedantry and mechanical rigidity versus flexibility and suppleness as the pedants collide with the ordinary people – labourers, sailors, water carriers, etc. This kind of linguistic masochism is still in evidence and the modern purists produced a new wave of hilarity, as when they insisted, for example, on arabizing the simple and universal word 'sandwich' into *al-shatir wa al-mashtur wa al-Kamikh baynahuma* (the slicer, the sliced and the cold meat in between them).

Next to the pedantry of the grammarians and rhetoricians, the *zurafa'* found another source of humour in the legal profession, which has lain almost as heavily with its rigidity on the chests and limbs of the common folk. A woman came once to the renowned Zarif Abu Dhamdham complaining of a man who kissed her and asked what she could do. Abu Dhamdham reminded her of the sacred principle of retribution in accordance with the Qur'anic verse, 'Injury shall be requited by retaliation.'[7] Therefore, 'You must kiss the man,' he told her.

The weakness and hypocrisy of the *qadis* (judges) was another subject which tickled the *zurafa'*. A young woman was delivered to a *qadi* as a ward of court and was, as customary, accommodated with his household. The following morning the judge was seen rushing out of his house and tearing his hair in disgust. 'Oh, there is no honesty left in this world. They delivered to me this maid as *virgo intacta*. I tried her and she was no virgin at all.'

Humour was the sport of Arab intellect, and both the reader and the writer accepted the fun in good part and with full recognition of the rules of the game. Within this milieu of innocence and purity, the *zarif* was free to make his comments and express himself. After some long verses in praise of wine, women and love, Muhammad Sa'id al-Habbubi, the Iraqi poet and religious *shaykh* of the nineteenth century, concluded thus:

O, do not be deceived, and those who listen are often   deceived,
   That my heart is longing for wine,
For a slim damsel with slumbering eyes,
   And figure which puts the straight spear to shame.
I only wanted to follow the example of the *zurafa'*:
   A wicked tongue with a virtuous soul.

Virtuous or sinful, the orthodox doctors were not amused and attacked this licentious treatment of dogma and establishment as a matter of trifling with religion and moral standards. As expected, they cited various authorities, genuine or faked, in support of their case against humour and wit. A contradictory saying was attributed to the Prophet to this effect: 'Beware of including laughing matter in your speech, even if in report of others.' Another saying was quoted from the pious Caliph of the Umayyad dynasty, Omar Ibn Abd al-Aziz: 'Raillery can only arise out of absurdity or discontentment.' The Muslims seem to have distinguished between *fukaha* (humour) which was permissible, and *mizah* (raillery) which was frowned upon, as in the advice of the second Caliph Omar Ibn al-Khattab: 'Prevent the people from raillery because it takes away kindness and puts anger in their hearts.' In similar vein Muhammad said, 'Avoid raillery because it takes away the dignity of the believer, destroys his kindness and arouses his anger.' And again, 'Raillery is the work of the devil and a product of sinfulness.'

The controversy between *al-mutazammitin* (the dogmatists) and the *zurafa'* continued. As the dogmatists criticized obscenity and the use of vulgar sexuality, Ibn Qutayba replied in his *Uyun al-Akhbar*, defending his own involvement in this trend:

This book is like a banqueting table on which is laid food with different flavours on account of the different palates of the eaters. Should you come across some account referring to private parts, vagina or a description of coitus, you should not, out of piety or piosity, raise your eyebrow and look askance, for there is no sin in mentioning the [sexual] organs. The sin is to defame honour, tell lies, give false witness and devour people's flesh in ignorance.

The two leading prose writers of the Abbasid era, Al-Jahiz and Ibn Abd Rabbih, defended humour, which the latter described as springtime to the hearts and recreation for the souls. The religious authority of al-Hasan al-Basri was quoted in evidence of the effectiveness and acceptance of *zarf*: 'If a thief is a *zarif*, his hands will not be cut off.'

However, Arab commentators on laughter seem to endorse the general line accepted by philosophers from Aristotle's days to our own time, i.e. that excessive humour is in bad taste and a harmful practice. Muslim thinkers were much influenced by Aristotle and his theory of the middle course which had led him to declare that he who indulges in laughter regardless of the price is a buffoon and he who rejects laughter is a boor. Wit, he had said in his *Ethics*, is a man whose pleasantries do not go too far. This corresponds to a great extent to al-Jahiz's advocacy of moderation: 'Jesting has a place and a measure. If anyone crossed the boundary or fell short, his excessiveness would be foul and his shortcoming would be a deficiency.' Yet, this spirit of moderation seems to have had an earlier history quite independent of the Aristotelian opinion, for the Prophet Muhammad, who loved and commended humour, said also, 'Avoid excessive laughter, because it kills the heart and causes forgetfulness.' Another saying to the same effect is attributed to al-Ahnaf: 'Dignity is destroyed with too much laughter and kindness is destroyed with too much jesting.'

Despite the rich legacy of Arab humour and the disputations and commentaries which went with it, no Arab thinker made any full examination of this subject. I have not seen any philosophic attempt to differentiate between the various forms of humour. Al-Tha'alibi made a nine-degrees classification of laughter according to its intensity from *tabassum* (smile) to *zahraqa* (to be totally over-whelmed with laughter), but no suggestion was made as to the method or style. Under the influence of modern Western thought and English literature, the Egyptian humourist, al-Mazini, discussed the subject and differentiated between *nukta* (joke) and *fukaha* (humour):

> The joke is a product of intuition and its scope is related, more often than not, to the apparent behaviour. Rarely does the joker go beyond the surface or dive into the distant depths. It makes us laugh by comparing two things, two conditions or behaviours. Humour is very different as it revolves around the meaning and truth, seeks the essence and ignores the apparent form. Thus, the difference is clear between the casual matter of the joke, and the carefully and profoundly examined matter of humour.[8]

One method of humour, however, seems to have attracted the

attention of the professional humourists, namely *qalb* (inversion). Abu al-Ibar, the court jester of the Abbasid Caliph al-Mutawakkil, was famous in this technique. By this time, humour and jest had become a craft to be learnt and Abu al-Ibar was apprenticed to one who was a master in this method and taught his pupils to say and do the opposite of what was expected, e.g. to say 'Good evening' in the morning, and 'Good morning' in the evening. One day, Abu al-Ibar went on to relate, he had written a letter and asked him to dry it for him with powder. Abu al-Ibar then poured water on it. 'What is this?' said the master.

'Aren't we supposed to do the opposite all day?' replied the pupil. The teacher then told him not to come any more. His apprenticeship was complete. It is a great pity that we have no record of what went on in such schools other than such scanty snippets.

More definite influence of Greek thought may easily be detected in the theorem of Arab physicians on the function of laughter. Like all doctors since the days of Plato and Aristotle, they endorsed the view that man's character rested on the equilibrium of the four body fluids or humours and that laughter or melancholy depended on the activity of the black bile. Al-Kindi gave a definition of laughter as 'an even-tempered purity of the blood of the heart together with an expansion of the soul to a point where its joy becomes visible. It has a physiological origin.'[9] Most Arab doctors supported the physiological roots of laughter. Writing in the ninth-century, Ishaq Ibn Umran traced its origin to the spleen or the liver which produced the blood and distributed the surplus between the yellow bile and the black bile, whereas the blood distributed by the heart was purer, thinner and better and carried less of the animal spirit. Ibn al-Matran (d. 1191) corroborated also the theory concerning the liver and the spleen and their even temper and discussed the good quality of blood as a source of joy, which in turn gives rise to laughter.

Notwithstanding this physiological hypothesis, Arab doctors tackled the phenomenon at the same time from the psychological angle, as was outlined in our introduction. Practically all of them viewed the subject from an optimistic angle, treating laughter as a sign of joy and a corrective factor, and many of them hit on the crucial element of astonishment and wonder. In his medical encyclopaedic work, *Firdaus al-Hikma* (The Paradise of Wisdom) Ali Ibn Rabban al-Tabari concluded that when a man hears or sees something unusual which diverts his mind and startles him, his blood begins to boil which, if the cause of the astonishment is not understood, results in laughter. In this function, the human being stands apart from other living beings as the only laughing animal. After drawing attention to laughter as another facet of the symptom of madness in his book *On Melancholy*, Ibn Imran defined laughter as astonishment of the soul as it beholds something it is not in a position to understand clearly.

It would be tedious to refer to the numerous works produced on this subject by Arab and Muslim physicians and the foregoing brief account is only meant as a pointer to the interest which humour has aroused in the minds of the philosophers and writers. Among the latter category, Abu Amr al-Jahiz (d. 869) stands out as probably the most lively and versatile writer of humour in the middle ages. His own visage, character, life and even death were something of the comic, as it was reported that he died as a result of his books falling on top of him. He was called al-Jahiz because his eyes were poking out of what must have been a grotesque face. He himself relates how a woman asked him to do her the favour of accompanying her to a goldsmith. 'Like that,' she said to the goldsmith, pointing at al-Jahiz. 'What is the meaning of this?' he enquired after the woman had gone. 'This woman,' said the goldsmith, 'brought me a stone and asked me to engrave on it the image of the devil. I told her I have never seen the devil, and so she brought you to me.'

Al-Jahiz wrote many books which are now classic literature, but they all share this preoccupation with the funny side of life, which had become almost an obsession with him. 'By God, I cannot leave out a joke even if it killed me in this world and sent me to hell in the next,' he wrote. In addition to his skill in storytelling and pursuit of details, he was a master caricaturist, as shown in his *Risalat al Tarbi' wa al-Tadwir* (The Letter of the Squared and the Circled) which runs to some 150 pages in drawing a satirical picture of one Ahmad Ibn Abd al-Wahhab. Perhaps al-Jahiz's most famous book is *Kitab al Bukhalá* (The Book of Misers) in which he included all kinds of anecdotes and epigrams about misers and miserliness underlining, from a sociological point of view, the poverty of the masses, the obsession with food and eating and the clash between the old Arab tradition of hospitality and generosity with the new city modes of life based on thrift, wealth, accumulation and security. The following are two samples from *The Book of Misers* which will be discussed in more detail in the next chapter:

– In answer to a question about the bravest man in the world, a miser replied, 'The man who hears other people's teeth on his food without bursting his gall bladder.'

– A doctor called on a mean friend and was told that his friend was suffering from a chill. 'Eat by his bedside until he sweats,' the doctor advised.

Next to the misers, the teachers made up the second category of people who amused al-Jahiz with their defects. 'Where would they learn any sense,' said one Arab wit, 'if they spend the day with children and the night with women!' Al-Jahiz mentioned that he had decided to shelve his book *Anecdotes on Teachers* after meeting a very reasonable teacher who impressed him with his tact and good sense and became a close friend of his. One day, however, he saw him in a sorry state of mourning. 'May God requite your pain, and may you find in the Messenger of God a worthy example. Every soul will meet death. Pray you, have patience. But this person who died – was it your son?'

He replied: 'No.'

'Was it your father then?'

Again he replied in the negative.

'Then was it your brother?'

It wasn't.

'Perhaps your wife? No? Then who was it?'

'My beloved,' said he.

This is the first ill-omen, al-Jahiz said to himself, and then continued, 'Glory be to Allah. Women are plentiful and you will soon find another.'

'Do you think I knew her?' he asked.

And this is the second ill-omen, al-Jahiz said to himself. 'Then How did you love someone you have never seen?'

The hapless teacher then related how, while resting under an archway, he heard a man murmuring:

O Um Amr. God reward your kindness,
Restore my heart to its former state!
Do not wrench it and play with it!
How can a human being play with another's life?

Hearing of such a bewitching beauty, the teacher fell in love with her and went on cherishing his romance until one day he heard a mournful voice chanting:

The donkey went away with Um Amr.
Neither she nor the donkey has ever come back.

Thus, he divined, his love must have died! Upon hearing this very sad story, al-Jahiz decided to go ahead and publish his book on the foolishness of the teaching fraternity.

Foolishness remained indeed a major theme in Arabic humorous literature and a few works have been written on the follies of fools. Again al-Jahiz included many of their stories like these:

– An *ahmaq* (fool) inherited half a house and proceeded to tell his friends, 'I tell you what. I shall sell my half and with the money I shall buy the other half and then the whole house will be mine.'

– A man asked his foolish servant, 'When did we make the Friday prayer at Risafa?' The servant thought for a long while and then said, 'It was probably on Tuesday.'

– An *ahmaq* heard that fasting the Day of Arafat is equivalent to the fasting of a whole year. He, therefore, fasted until lunch time and said, 'Six months are sufficient for me.'

– Two rascals conspired to rob a fool of his donkey. One of them removed the rein from its neck and put it around his own neck and followed the fool, while the other made off with the beast. After a while, the fool stopped and was surprised to find at the end of the rein a man and not an animal.

'I am your donkey,' said the rascal. 'I was troublesome to Mother and God turned me into an ass and I served you all these years. Now Mother must have forgiven me, and so God has restored me to my former self.'

'There is no power or means other than Allah's,' said the fool as he freed the man and went home to atone for his sin in using a man as a donkey. A few days later he went to the market to look for a new beast, and there he saw the same donkey for sale.

'Oh you terror!' whispered the fool into the donkey's ear, 'Again you tormented you mother!'

The names of many fools like Hubannaq and Bahlul, whose escapades were of great popularity in Baghdad in the eighteenth century as was noted by the European traveller Niebuhr during his visit to the city, acquired a lasting fame, but the most famous name which has become a universal legend is that of Juha, the mercurial fool with his tantalizing follies and teasing wisdom. Al-Jahiz wrote for the literate élite; Juha spoke for and to the general masses, expressing their cynicism and frustration.

– Seeing the people praying and repenting during a violent storm he called on them, 'Oh, good people don't rush and repent! It is only a storm which will soon pass.'

– He was asked which was more useful – the sun or the moon. 'The moon without any doubt', he said. 'The sun comes out during the day when it's not needed.'

– Travelling with his son and having only one donkey, he could do nothing but allow his son to ride while he walked behind. The people sneered at them, 'What a spoilt brat. Riding and leaving his old father to walk!' Juha stopped and reversed the order, but another group of people saw them and remarked, 'What a selfish father, riding and leaving his poor child to struggle.' Juha stopped again and decided this time that they should both ride, but still they could not escape the censure. 'Look at this cruel lot! Both of them riding on this poor animal!' Juha stopped once more. This time they both walked. 'How stupid! Travelling on foot when they have a free donkey with them.' Juha stopped for the last time. 'My son, the only way left to satisfy the people is to carry the beast ourselves. Help me with it!' Juhu and son continued their journey carrying the donkey to the roaring laughter and sneers of the onlookers.

The Arabs feel really at home in the past and like their favourite animal – the camel – they have an uncanny knack for mental regurgitation. Most literate Arabs can and do cite a sixth-century verse with the same ease of an English actor in citing Shakespeare. In all probability most of the jokes and anecdotes narrated in this chapter are a reprint of earlier versions. With the same process of regurgitation and adaptation, our contemporary humorists, politicians, caricaturists and columnists recycled, in varying degrees, the humorous treasures of the past to serve the political slogans and aspirations of the present.

'Mr Egyptian: "Labour Leaders in Britain have sunk their differences and
  joined their opponents. What about you?"
Egypt's Leaders: "They are poor labourers. We are Pashas."'
Sarukhan, *Akhir Sa'a* 1939.

2 Political Humour in Arab History

> When raillery is calculated to benefit and laughter is used
> for its proper aim, raillery becomes instructive and laughter
> dignified.
>
> Al-Jahiz

Despite the wealth of humorous literature on one hand, and the
continuous conflicts which filled Arab history, we are left with very
little to show on the ledger of political humour. This is understandable in view of the despotic style of the medieval government
and the fact that most writers were attached to this or that prince
who enjoyed, in the Muslim world, religious as well as secular
authority. When they did report a discordant matter, it was usually
about some bygone period or the ruler of an opposing camp. The
jokes which must have been in circulation among the masses went
mostly unrecorded, but one story quoted by the historian, al-Tabari,
gives us an idea of the general interest in political matters. Abu
al-Hasan Ibn Ayyash related that he saw in the streets of Baghdad a
busker with a monkey. The busker was asking the monkey whether
he would like to be a cloth merchant, a grocer, a tradesman, etc., and
the ape was nodding his head every time in delighted approval until
he was asked whether he wanted to be a minister. The monkey then
filled the place with horrified shrieks and ran amok pretending to be
running for his life. It is noteworthy that the busker mentioned the
minister and not the caliph, a practice which was often repeated by
the satirists in their attacks against the government. In their
characteristic insubordination and individualism, the Arabs have
exhibited a dislike for and suspicion of rulers, but whenever they
had the caliph in mind, they preferred to substitute 'sultan' or 'king'
for the prince of the believers and successor (caliph) of the
Messenger of God. Thus it was reported in *Risalat al-Ghuphran* that
a sultan's companion saw a philosopher picking weeds for food and
said to him, 'If you served the kings, you wouldn't need to eat weeds.'

The philosopher answered, 'If you ate weeds, you wouldn't need to serve kings.' There is a wealth of proverbs and anecdotes advising the listener to shun the ruler's court as if it were a cesspit of vice and villainy. A common proverb in the form of a prayer simply says: 'No ruler and no doctor' (*la hakim wa la hakeem*). The following are some examples of the common sayings currently in use:

- The sultan is the one who knows no sultan.
- Like the whips of the ruler, what miss you are better than what reach you.
- He who eats from the sultan's gravy will have his lip split.
- O, Pharoah, what made you a pharoah? He said, 'The lack of any one opposing me.'
- If you want something from a dog, call him, 'sir'!
- Bribe and Prosper.
- The bribe is a big boss.
- No one dares say to a soldier, 'Cover up your beard.'

In yet another story given in *Muhadharat al-Raghib*, a water-carrier approaches a *faqih* (theologian) at the gates of a sultan and asks him a question. 'Is this the place to ask me?' says the *faqih*. 'Is this the place for a faqih to be found in?' answers the water-carrier.

Sometimes, writers attributed their stories, rightly or wrongly, to foreign rulers as Abu Hayan al-Tawhidi did in his anecdote of the usurped estate. A man complained to the King of Persia about his admiral who seized his land.

'How long have you had it?'

The man explained that he had inherited it from his father and grandfather.

'You have used it for a long time. Why not lend it to the admiral to enjoy it for a few years?' said the king.

'Your majesty is aware of the good work of Baramjur in your service and your father's service,' said the landowner. 'Why not lend him your kingdom to enjoy for a few years, and then he will restore it to you.'[1]

The Islamic Empire extended from Spain to India and China and the caliph was soon forced to concede in most territories all but his nominal authority in the form of the Friday prayer to wish him well. The average citizen had to contend with the local *walis* (governors) and *qadis* (judges) who slipped gradually into more and more corruption, vice and tyranny, especially after the rise of the Ottoman Empire and its domination over Arab lands. Against such figures of officialdom, the ordinary people directed their wrath, clothed in cynical jibes and sarcasm. The picture can be invoked from present day practice. In most Arab villages and poor urban districts, there is often some 'village jester' who lives on his 'wit' by roaming the bazaars and cafés, amusing the people with his anecdotes, jokes and epigrams, about the local constable, municipal inspector, district officer, etc. I remember such a person, an unemployed porter, at the little holy town of Kazimia, just north of Baghdad. One of his remarks which stuck in my mind was his reply to my question about teeth and the condition of his own teeth. 'Oh, they are all right, sir. Why should anything happen to them – when am I ever using them?' He once saw a policeman chasing some school kids after a demonstration. 'What is the matter?'

'The buggers! They want to topple the government,' answered the policeman.

'Topple the government? Do you think our government is a barrel of shit?' he remarked in dishonest disgust. Among the anecdotes he related was the one about Abbas, the illiterate local cop. He suspected a young man standing at the river front of the criminal intention of distributing leaflets. So he interrogated him: 'Why are you standing here?'

'Oh, just looking at the landscape.'

'What landscape?'

'This lovely moon, the river, the palm trees . . .'

'Yes, yes. I see the moon, I see the river, the palm trees, but where is the landscape?'

For the price of a kebab sandwich and a little friendliness and understanding, you could have the company of such men to entertain you well into the small hours of the morning in any non-oil-producing country. Similar stories, however, were indeed recorded against the police, the judges, governors, and officers of the sultan. It was thus said that during his brief visit to paradise, the Prophet Muhammad was surprised to see a wolf. 'A wolf in paradise?' the Messenger of God asked the animal.

'Yes, I ate a policeman's son,' answered the wolf.

'That for eating the son of a policeman!' commented one of the *zurafá*. 'Had he eaten the policeman himself, he would have been put in the highest heaven.'

Abu Abbad, the secretary of the Caliph al-Ma'mun, gave an account of a delegation which called on the caliph, begging him to remove his *wali* from their town, Kufa. 'In his first year, we sold our furniture and lands. In the second year, we disposed of our heirlooms and states, and in the third year we left our town and sought the aid of the Prince of the Believers that he might in mercy redress our

grievance and remove him.' Al-Ma'mun objected to their protestation
and affirmed the good conduct, religion and honesty of his *wali*. 'O,
Prince of the Believers,' their representative went on, 'you have
spoken the truth and we have told a lie. But as for this *wali* whose
religion, honesty, continence, justice and equity you have approved,
why have you assigned him to us exclusively all these years and not
to a country with the care of the affairs of which God has entrusted
you equally with ours? Employ him therefore in that country so that
his justice and equity may extend to the people there as it did to us.'

The corruption of the *qadis* and *walis* and their ingenious devices
for extracting money from the citizenry became and remained a
fertile ground for the humour of the *zurafá*. A *wali* newly appointed
for Bahrain was visited, as was customary, by the leaders of the
various denominations. 'What did you do to Christ the son of Mary?'
he asked the Jews.

'We killed him,' they replied.

'By God, you will stay in prison until you pay his *diyya* (blood
money).'

In another story, the Jews had a better spokesman. The new *wali*
tethered a goat at his court and asked the *imam*, the representative
of the Muslim community: 'What do you think of my pet?'

'Indeed, Your Excellency, it is a very fine goat.'

'A goat?' shouted the *wali*, 'you want to denigrate the person of the
wali by calling his gazelle a goat! By Allah, you will have to pay a
thousand liras in fines, or you go to gaol.'

The following day it was the turn of the Christians whose bishop
had his tip from the *imam*. 'Indeed, Your Excellency, it is a very fine
gazelle,' said the bishop.

'What!' shouted the *wali*, 'Are you taking me for a fool – calling it a
gazelle when anyone can see it is only a goat? By Allah, you will pay a
thousand liras, or you go to gaol.'

Next day, the rabbi had his tip from the bishop. 'Your Excellency,
this is neither a goat nor a gazelle but a hungry monster who can
only be pacified with this,' and the rabbi produced his sack of gold
which he delivered without further ado.

'You are a very wise man', said the *wali*, 'and I shall always rely on
your good counsel.'

Such anecdotes were much in evidence under the Ottoman rule
and served as a wonderful source of political criticism and
moralization after independence. A Jewish merchant spat at
the face of a Muslim agent and the agent took him to the Turkish
judge for abusing the face of a Muslim and quenching the light of

Islam radiating from it.

'I have a *firman* (Royal Decree) from the sultan to spit at his face,' said the Jew.

'How is that? Show it to me then,' said the *qadi*.

The merchant then handed the court a folder wherein the *qadi* saw a banknote neatly filed. 'Yes, it is too true, my dear fellow,' said the *qadi* to the plaintiff, 'this Jew has a *firman* which gives him the right to spit not only at your face, but also at my face and the face of the sultan himself. The case is dismissed.'

During the decline of the Arab Empire, which began from the tenth century, the storyteller of the *Maqamat*, Badi'al-Zaman al-Hamathani, described in rhymed prose one of the judges of this period, Abu Bakr al-Hayri al-Qadi.

Justice was entrusted to one who has none of its qualifications other than his moustache, and knows none of its means except his own isolation. Usurpation of rights is the sole import of his judgements; break-up of families is all that he understands of parting; the acquisition of wealth is his mastery of jurisprudence. In religious duties, he only excels in dissimulation and extreme affectation. In the fields of disputation, he studies only falsehood and misdeeds. This is Abu Bakr al-Qadi – may God annihilate him as he has annihilated trust and betrayed the treasury... Is it not sufficient that he was one who started his mornings between the wine jar and the lute and his evenings with the cardinal sins until his youth was over and his hair locks turned grey and then he put on his judge's cap and smoothed his cloak to deviate both his hand and his tongue, trim his moustache, lengthen his ropes, exhibit his pains to camouflage his follies, whiten his beard to blacken his record, assume piety to conceal his greed, stand at the altar to stuff his sack, augment his prayers to fill up his jar and serve his belly by day and treat its discomfort at night.

May the Almighty curse this *qadi* who finds no evidence before him stronger than bribery and liquor submitted to the court, no authentication more genuine than gold dancing at his fingertips, no document closer to his heart than the eyes of the opponents winking at the tied money bag, no guarantor more creditable than the secret final gift and the loaded night porter, no attorney dearer to him than the handkerchief and the plate delivered in the evening or in the morning, no government more hateful than that of council, no case less exciting than that of a bankrupt ...

How do you expect knowledge to come to one who spent his boyhood in fornication, his youth on his belly, his days on grabbing and his nights in intercourse, interrupted his felicity with riches and his solitude with singing, and emptied his solemnity in his bag and his humour in his glass?[2]

Already during the government of the Rashidin caliphs of early Islam, Ali Ibn Abi Talib, the pious fourth caliph, was conscious of the frailty of justice when he expressed his anger at the way things were going. 'A case may be submitted to one of them on one of the points of law and he pronounces his verdict. Then the same case is put before another judge who gives a contradictory verdict. The judges then refer the case to the *imam* who appointed them and the *imam* approves of both judgements.'

Ali Ibn Abi Talib was one of the most eloquent orators whose sayings and epigrams are still recalled by Muslims throughout the world. He was once asked about the *ghawgha'* (mobs). 'They are people who are harmful when they gather and useful when they disperse,' he answered. One of his opponents pretended love and went on praising him until he was interrupted by Ali, 'I am below what you are saying and above what is in your mind.' His caliphate was troubled with the great schism which rocked the course of Islam and continues to this day. The conflict erupted between him at the head of the Hashimites and Mu'awiya at the head of the Umayyads. The former set up his camp in Iraq and the latter in Syria and the feud between the two regions continued. The Iraqis are brave people and noted for their violence and aggressiveness, but they had long lost the readiness to sacrifice their blood for rulers and prophets and preferred to retain their valour for themselves, each defending his own. The god-fearing and politically naïve Ali had therefore great trouble in stirring them to fight for the Hashimite cause. His frustation inspired him to great speeches full of sarcasm:

If I order you to march on them on warm days, you say, 'This is the fire of the summer. Give us time until the heat is over.' If I ask you to march on them on a winter morning you say, 'This is the bite of the frost – give us time until the cold is over.' All this and you fleeing from the heat and the cold, but by God, you are more in flight from the sword.

The conflict became more intense and the two camps eventually joined in battle. Just when Ali gained the upper hand over his adversary, Amr Ibn al-As, and was about to kill him, Amr resorted to his cunning and the Arabic cynical saying 'Flight is two thirds of valour,' and turned his back to Ali exposing his bottom, whereupon the caliph drew back his sword. Drama turned to farce and the caliph gave the only appropriate report. 'The son of the infamous woman! What a master and commander when he is about the war as long as the swords are in their sheaths. But once they are out, his greatest device is to turn his arse towards the people.' Ali's critics were not amused and blamed the caliph for his proud chivalry and lack of determination. Amr Ibn al-As accused him of triviality and childish play. His brother Aqil took his goat and went to visit him to reason with him in vain. 'One of the three of us must be a fool,' Ali said to Aqil in the heat of the argument. 'Well, it's not I nor my goat,' replied his brother.[3]

The good caliph was eventually murdered in the mosque and the issue deepened the turmoil of Islam. Years later, an Iraqi pilgrim told the Qadi of Mecca that the flies were troubling him in the great mosque of Qa'ba and asked whether it was all right in the eyes of God to kill a fly in His house. The *qadi* replied, 'You people of Iraq had the godly imam Ali, the Prince of the Believers, the Successor of the Prophet, his own cousin and son-in-law among you, and while making his prayers in the mosque, you killed him. I suppose you shouldn't worry too much now about killing a fly.'

After Ali's death, the conflict continued between Hasan, his son and Mu'awiya. In an encounter between the two opponents, Hasan started by recalling the Prophet's curse upon the gluttonous Mu'awiya, 'May Allah never appease the craving of thy belly!' and went on to answer Mu'awiya's charges by telling the story of the gnat and the palm tree. 'You, Mu'awiya, resemble that gnat which settled on a palm tree. The gnat cried out to the tree, "Hold fast, for I am going to take off." The palm tree replied to her, "I was not even aware of your presence, so how could your taking off harm me?" And how, O you one-eyed *thakafi*, could your charges affect me?'[4]

Ali's stoic piety, summed up in his words, 'To me, your world is not worth the fart of a goat,' was in total contrast to the luxury and wealth which the Umayyads considered as the rightful due of the victorious Arabs. The Caliph Omar Ibn al-Khattab was horrified when he heard of the assets accumulated by Amr Ibn al-As, his governor over Egypt, and sent his auditor to check and prepare an inventory of his possessions. 'An age in which the son of Hantama treats us thus is certainly an evil age,' said the governor.

'Hush,' replied the inspector, 'had it not been due to this age of the son of Hantama which you hate, you would be today bending in the courtyard of your house, at the feet of a goat whose abundance of milk would please you or whose scarcity would cause you dismay.'

The Iraqis who killed Imam Ali and betrayed his son, Imam Hussein, decided to make amends for their former sins by verbal means, of course. Endless poems and anecdotes were circulated and compiled in condemnation of the Umayyads. It was thus reported that when Buthaina, the heroine of the famous Jamil and Buthaina romance, called on the Caliph Abd al-Malik Ibn Marwan in her old age, he said to her, 'Damn you! What did Jamil see in you?'

'That which the nation saw in you when they entrusted you with their affairs,' she replied.

In another anecdote about him, we are told that he was once separated from his followers during a hunt, and came across a Bedouin.

'Do you know who am I?'

'Yes, a despot and son of a debauchee.'

'How dare you? I am Abd al-Malik Ibn Marwan.'

'May God never greet you or bring you near. You have robbed God's funds and violated His sanctity.'

'How dare you? I can do harm and can bring benefits.'

'May God never endow me with your benefits or protect me from your harm.'

The royal entourage soon caught up with the caliph and the helpless Bedouin could only think of whispering in the ear of Abd al-Malik: 'Pray you, Prince of the Believers, keep what I told you confidential between us.'

The caliph was amused and rewarded the man for his wit.

While Abd al-Malik was accused of despotism, his brother, Mu'awiya, was accused of stupidity as illustrated in the following story. Seeing a flour mill operated by a donkey turning around with a bell around his neck, he asked the miller about the function of the bell. 'I may get overcome with slumber or boredom. But once I notice that the bell has stopped ringing, I know that the donkey has stopped, and then I shoo him to make him move.'

Mu'awiya then asked, 'What if the donkey stops and only shakes his head this way and that way. How will you know that he has stopped?'

The miller had only one answer: 'Wherefrom can my donkey acquire a brain like that of the prince?'

Caliphs were usually given high-sounding titles, but two of the Umayyad caliphs were nicknamed Walid the Drunkard and Marwan the Ass.

The Umayyads were harassed on many fronts and the caliph had to do battle in many directions. After subduing the revolt of Hijaz, Abd al-Malik went to Medina and spoke to its people telling them of the fable of the two brothers and the snake which came out every morning with a golden dinar. The two brothers became more covetous and decided to kill the snake and possess the whole treasure, but their blow only injured its head and the snake countered by fatally biting one of them. After a while, the surviving brother regretted his deed. 'By God, I wasn't happy with what happened to you,' he said to the snake, 'and warned my brother against it. Can we now put God between us that I may not hurt you and you may not hurt me, and you resume your former practice?'

'Oh, no,' said the snake. 'I know you'll never be well disposed towards me as you see your brother's grave, and I'll never be well disposed towards you as I remember this fracture in my head.'

The caliph then reminded Quraish how they had killed Uthman and how the Umayyads avenged his death in the Harra massacre. 'You'll never love us as you remember the Day of Harra and we'll never love you as we remember the murder of Uthman.'

Thus no love was lost between the ruler and his subjects and Abd al-Malik's next move was to despatch his ruthless commander, al-Hajjaj, to subdue the rebellious Iraqis. Like most other Arab commanders, al-Hajjaj was a great orator steeped in the tradition of Arabic poetry, eloquence and sarcastic humour. The scene of his reception at the Mosque of Kufa is learnt by all school children in Iraq and many other parts of the Arab world. The congregation booed, swore and even threw stones at the new *wali* who sat calmly and silently for a few minutes before ordering the guards to close all the doors of the mosque. He then introduced himself with a telling verse:

I am the disperser of all doubt, the climber of mountains.
When I put on my helmet, you will know me.

As for his mission, he looked at the people before him and put it thus: 'I see some heads which have ripened and become due for picking. I shall be their picker! O people of Kufa, I look and see as if blood is streaming between the turbans and the beards.' Resorting to the effective rhyming which has always thrilled the Arabs and made them believe that what they heard was actually true, he described the people of Iraq as the people of *shiqaq* and *nifaq* (dissention and dissimulation) and the description has stuck to them ever since.

Oh, people of Iraq, Satan has gone inside you, penetrated your flesh and blood, your nerves, your ears, your limbs, your organs, your hearts' tissues, and mixed with your bone marrow and eardrums. He then went up and built a nest, laid his eggs, hatched them and produced the dissention and dissimulation which filled you up and bent you on schism. You have adopted him as your mentor to follow, your leader to obey and your commander to consult.

The Iraqis could do nothing against his iron-fist rule other than pray to God to take him, a hope which they eventually fulfilled by wishful rumouring when they spread the news that al-Hajjaj was dead. The following day, he went up to the pulpit and delivered another piece of sick humour:

I have not seen God granting immortality except to the worst of his creations: the devil ... By Allah, I look at you as if every living man among you is a dead man, and every supple one a stiff one, carried in his shroud to a pit three arms-lengths long and one arm-length wide, where the earth eats up his flesh and sucks up his pus. The beloved of his sons depart to divide the wicked of his wealth.

Al-Hajjaj left a lasting mark on Iraq and despite all the revulsion they feel against him and his rule, you will often hear them utter in their political despair, their time-honoured saying, 'What we need is a Hajjaj.' However, in their frustration in dealing with him, the Iraqis had only political humour left in their hands and went on to invent stories about him. Ibn Khallikan cites the anecdote of a man who swore an oath that his wife would be divorced from him if al-Hajjaj did not end up in hell. Realizing the seriousness of his oath, that he might live in sin with his wife if God's verdict on the hated *wali* went the other way, he went to consult Ibn Ubaid, the *imam* of the Mu'tazila sect. Ibn Ubaid gave him this judgement: 'Stay with you wife, for if the Most High forgives al-Hajjaj, there won't be any harm in your fornication.'

In a similar episode like that of Abd al-Malik, Ibn Qutaiba related that al-Hajjaj went on an outing, and was by himself when he spoke to an old man and asked him what he thought of his country's rulers.

'They are all evil men, ruling the people with injustice and robbing them of their possessions.'

'And what do you think of al-Hajjaj?'

'He is the worst of them all, may God disgrace his face and the faces of those who employed him here.'

'Do you know who I am?'

'No, by God.'

'I am al-Hajjaj!'

The old man looked at him with dismay, thought for a while and then smiled. 'Do you know who I am?'

'No.'

'I am Bani Ajil's *majnun* (lunatic). I lose my senses once a day at about this time.'

Like Abd al-Malik, al-Hajjaj was also amused and gave the old peasant some reward. Arab humourists seem to enjoy this kind of encounter in which the emperor is stripped of his clothes and the subject is rid of his fears.

A more recent story was related to me about King Faisal, the founder of modern Iraq and his renowned Prime Minister, Nuri al-Sa'id. New to Iraq and as poor as a church mouse, Faisal asked al-Sa'id how the people in Baghdad spent their leisure time. The Prime Minister told him that nocturnal river trips by rowing-boat were the prime pleasure of Baghdad. The King expressed his desire to experience this and al-Sa'id hired a boat for the purpose. Under cover of darkness, the two slipped away unknown to Da'bul the boatman who, like most of his colleagues, was in the habit of drinking *arak* every night. As a true Baghdadi, he offered the hospitality of the bottle and the King, being a true Arab, could not decline hospitality, but being also a good Muslim, he only put the bottle to his lips and passed it on to his Prime Minister. Nuri al-Sa'id, a great lover of the national liquor, took a sip and returned the bottle to the boatman who, having thus made himself agreeable to the two gentlemen, went on to entertain them with his conversation, which in Iraq simply meant grumbling about the government, swearing at its ministers and postulating grand new ideas on how best to put everything right. As the trip came to its end, al-Sa'id asked the boatman, 'Do you know who I am?'

'Not in the least,' replied the man.

'I am the Prime Minister of Iraq.'

Faisal hastened to add: 'And I am actually the King of Iraq.'

'Buzz off, you buggers,' snapped Da'bul, 'you had just one sip and you began to see yourself as our Prime Minister, and you had just half a sip and you saw yourself the King of Iraq. Get off my boat.'

The following day, Nuri al-Sa'id wanted to provide His Majesty with more amusement and sent for the boatman who used to ply his trade by the side of the Royal Palace at the Midan. In the course of the friendly exchange al-Sa'id asked him whether there was anything worthy of note on the river.

'Oh, not much, but I must tell you of these two good-for-nothing guys who . . .'

Al-Sa'id pretended to be angry at the story and ordered the guards to look for them.

'Oh, don't trouble yourself, Pasha. I can assure you, they were an utterly useless pair of rascals whom I wouldn't employ to make me a cup of tea.'

A story in a similar vein was recorded in *al-Mustatraf** about the Caliph al-Mahdi who had to accept the hospitality of an Arab peasant during a hunting expedition. The peasant gave him barley bread, some yoghurt and then wine. After one mug, al-Mahdi asked him, 'Do you know who I am?'

The peasant said that he did not and the caliph had to inform him modestly, 'I am one of the special servants of the Prince of the Believers.'

'May God bless you in your position,' added the host, as he replenished his mug with more wine which the caliph gulped gratefully and returned to his question, 'Do you know who I am?'

'You've just said that you are a special servant of the caliph.'

'No, I am one of the Commanders of the Prince of the Believers.'

The man lost no time in pouring him more wine, which the caliph drank and again repeated his question.

'You've said you are a Commander of the Prince of the Believers,' replied the man.

'No. I am the Prince of the Believers himself.'

The peasant kicked the mug away from him. 'By God, if you drink the fourth you will say you are the Messenger of God.'

The dissimulation and tact of the urban citizenry are contrasted by the direct retort and sharp wit of the Bedouins. Following the eventual overthrow of the Umayyads by the Abbasids, the boot was put on the other foot and Syria became the hotbed for the caliphate. In Damascus, the second Abbasid caliph, al-Mansur, wanted to pacify the restive subjects. 'Oh, people you should praise the Most High that He has given you my reign. For in fact, since I began to reign over you, the Almighty has taken away the plague which had spread among you.'

A Bedouin listener interjected, 'Truly, Allah is merciful. He

---

*A classic work of humour and literary entertainment by al-Abshihi

wouldn't have us suffer both you and the plague at the same time.'

In another anecdote, a man was arrested for carrying an empty jar of liquor and the *wali* ordered that he should be flogged. 'It was only an empty jar. Why are you flogging me?' said the man.

'Because you were carrying the instrument of liquor,' replied the *wali*.

'And you, may God give you strength, aren't you carrying with you the instrument of fornication?'

As the sinful habit of drinking became widespread, the subject of alcohol produced another genre of anti-clerical jokes. When al-Mansur wanted to reward the poet Ibrahim Ibn Harma, he asked him to name his wish.

'Write to your governor in Medina not to punish me if they find me drunk.'

The caliph explained that this was not possible, and the poet then said that he had no other wish. The caliph solved the problem by writing to his governor: 'If they bring Ibn Harma before you for drunkenness, give him eight strokes and give the policeman who brings him one hundred strokes.'

In another anecdote, a *zarif* heard a Christian describe paradise according to the teaching of the church – that in it there was no eating, drinking or sex. The *zarif* commented, 'This is the exact description of misery, sorrow and calamity.'

Arabic books are full of negative anecdotes and poems satirizing al-Mansur and especially his meanness for a very understandable reason. Arab writers and poets lived (and many of them still do) on the gifts and sustenance of the rulers. Al-Mansur was the builder of the metropolis of Baghdad and probably needed every ounce of gold for his ambitious enterprise. As expected, artists were and are less interested in development projects than in pursuing their own creative work. Therefore, they resented his tight-fisted treatment and called him al-Dawaniqi (*danaq* is the smallest denomination coin). Historians mention that on his pilgrimage to Mecca, he paid the singer, Muslim al-Hawi, half a dirham for singing him on his way. Al-Hawi protested, 'By Allah, I sang for al-Hisham and he rewarded me with thirty thousand dirhams.'

The caliph observed: 'You took from the Muslims' treasury thirty thousand dirhams! Rabi,' he called his secretary, 'appoint someone to recover this money from him.'

Al-Hawi had to pay back the money by singing him all the way from Baghdad to Mecca and back. It was no wonder that the poet, Muslim bin Yazid al-Adawi found it necessary to lampoon the caliph with a poem in which he said:

> Woe to men from the disease which has no antidote,
> And from the blind leader leading a blind mob!

The plight of the poets may be judged from al-Asma'i's story of the caliph who used a devilish device to trick the poets out of their traditional rewards. It was reported that al-Mansur had the gift of remembering a whole poem upon hearing it just once, and had also a *mamluk* (male servant) who could remember the poem upon hearing it twice, and a *jaria* (female slave) who could remember it upon hearing it thrice. When a poet came to the court to recite his new work and receive his reward, al-Mansur would protest, 'Why – this is not a new poem. I know it myself.' He would then recite it to the poor poet. By the time he had finished, the *mamluk* would have heard it twice. 'And even my *mamluk* here knows it. 'Recite it to him!' the caliph would say, and would move on after the third recital to call upon the *jaria* to demonstrate her former knowledge of the work. Frustrated and bewildered, the poet would then beg for his leave, to the laughter of the entire court.

Al-Asma'i, the versatile author and man of letters, did not share the general amusement and felt sorry for the plight of the poets. He therefore decided to rectify the situation by a counter-trick in which he composed a very difficult qasida which ran like this:

> By the piping voice of the Bulbul, by water and by
>   flowers,
> By the glint of a twinkling eye, by thee, O my master,
> My chieftain and my lord, the lover's heart is moved.
> How often has enslaved me, the gazelle of Ukekeelee,
> From off whose cheek by a kiss, I have culled the blushing
>   rose,
> Saying, Kiss, O! kiss, O! kiss me. But she sped not to embrace
>   me,
> And cried, No. No. No, no; then rose and quickly fled me
> To the caresses of this man, the maiden yielded tremblingly,
> And crying cried a cry, Woe! ah woe! ah woe is me!
> – Lament not this, I said, rather reveal thy pearls.

Neither this nor any other translation can convey the tongue-twisting quality and impossible construction of the original. Having disguised himself he went to the royal palace asking for permission to read a new poetic work. This was granted and the caliph was dumbfounded by the bewildering *qasida* and could not recall one single line. He looked at his *mamluk* and then at his *jaria* and could draw only blank looks from them, leaving him with no option but to pay up. 'Give us the piece of parchment to weigh it for you in gold, as customary,' said the caliph.

Al-Asma'i was expecting this question and prepared his answer: 'Alas, Prince of the Believers, I could find nothing to write my *qasida* on other than this column of marble which I have brought with me here.' The massive column was hauled in and the treasurer had to weigh it in gold, which pretty well left nothing in the royal coffers. Al-Mansur was intrigued and could not rest until he had sent his men after the masked poet to discover his identity, whereupon they found he was none but old Asma'i, who returned with them to the caliph to deliver these gentle and wise words: 'O, Prince of the Believers, verily the poets are poor people and are fathers of families, and you debar them from receiving anything by the power of your memory and the memory of this *mamluk* and this *jaria*. But were you to bestow upon them what you could easily spare, they might with it support their families without causing you any injury.'

Al-Mansur's meanness inspired, as was reported, at least two major works in Arabic literature, or indeed world literature. The first was al-Jahiz's *Book of Misers*; the second was Ibn al-Muqaffa's fables of *Kalila and Dimna*. The former, which caricatured notorious misers and spotlighted the evils and futility of meanness, has already been discussed and more will be said about its nationalistic aspects later; the latter had been originally written in Sanskrit and later translated into Pahlevi, from which Abdulla Ibn al-Muqaffa' adapted his Arabic version. Comparison between the two versions reveals distinct anti-establishment angles in al-Muqaffa's *Kalila and Dimna*. The moral fables, which have been translated repeatedly into English and other foreign languages, start by telling the adventure story of the brothers Kalila and Dimna, two jackals 'endowed with cleverness, science and culture', and the king of the jungle, 'a lion obsessed with his own opinion, unwilling to heed anybody's advice'. Noticing the lion's sudden withdrawal and anxiety caused by the roar of a strange bull, the scheming and ambitious jackal, Dimna, decides to approach the king and smooth his way into his heart by praising and encouraging anything he liked. 'And when he didn't like something and worried about its defects and harm, I would point out the defects and harm and advise him of the benefits and good resulting from the foregoing of it . . . The clever and sensitive man can, when he wishes, make right wrong and wrong right, just like the skilful painter who can paint pictures on the walls and make them look prominent when they are not, or depressed when they are not depressed.' Kalila warns him. 'Three things are attempted only by fools: keeping company with kings, trusting women with secrets, and drinking poison for experiment.' It is interesting to note how Ibn al-Muqaffa' removed in his version the Pahlevi advice, 'We are the King's servants and our business is to wait upon him and obey his orders.'[5]

However, Dimna did not listen to his brother's advice and joined the king of the jungle. The first trick was to relieve the king of his fears by presenting the harmless bull to him. Impressed by the size and loud voice of the beast, the king took him as his first counsellor, to the discomfiture of the jackal. Now how to dislodge the stupid bull as a favourite of the king was the jackal's next trick, which he hatched by conspiring with the wolf and the crow to convince the lion that the bull was plotting to overthrow him. Easily persuaded, the lion fought the innocent beast and killed him. Soon the lion regretted his haste and put the fox in prison. In the trial, the master pig came to testify against him by virtue of his privileged position in the court, but Dimna impeached his evidence. 'You limping, disfigured pig, with your bandy legs, blown-up belly, dangling testicles and split lips, ugly in both appearance and utterance!'

The master pig shrank, felt embarrassed and began to cry.

'Yea, you should cry long so that the king may see your squalor and faults and keep you away from his table, his service and his presence.'

One wonders what courtier the writer had in mind when he drew this character, or whether there was a prototype for it at all. The fox, however, was finally convicted and executed by the testimonies of two good witnesses – the leopard and the tiger.

The story and the stories inside the story rolled on and on. Al-Mansur and his royal entourage were not blind to the full significance of Ibn al-Muqaffa's work and the caliph availed himself of the first opportunity of having the gifted artist executed. Al-Muqaffa' seems to have inherited an anti-government strain from his father, who was imprisoned and tortured by al-Hajjaj.

Ibn al-Muqaffa's advice to shun the sultan was followed by at least one sensible man when al-Mansur wanted to appoint him as his *qadi*. The *faqih* apologized for not having the qualifications of a judge, upon which the caliph said, 'You are telling a lie, for you are one of the best men in the epoch.'

'That proves my point, O Prince of the Believers, for you have testified that I am a liar.'

Al-Mansur's military officers were also vilified as in this report. A prisoner-of-war taken from the Khawarij insurgents was brought before him and the caliph asked him about his own commanders and which of them had shown particular courage. 'I do not know them by their faces for I saw only their backs,' said the Khawariji.

After al-Mansur's death, Arab supremacy began to decline with the entry and assimilation of millions of non-Arab Muslims, bringing with them different traditions and cultures leading to the inevitable social tensions and conflicts. Al-Ma'mun, the son of Harun al-Rashid, filled the administration with Persians, and his brother, al-Mu'tasim, recruited the bulk of his army from the Turks, to whom the population took particular exception. Al-Mu'tasim lacked also the cultural interest which his learned brother had shown, a decline which was quickly noticed and resented by the fraternity of the poets and writers. Therefore they publicized the notion that the new caliph was uncouth and stupid, and circulated stories in evidence. It was thus reported that as a young prince, al-Mu'tasim used to go to school with another lad from the palace, who fell ill and died. Harun al-Rashid conveyed the sad news to his son. 'Yes, my Lord,' said the prince, 'but at least he is now at rest and does not have to go to school any more.'

'Is school as bad as that?' asked the caliph, and ordered that his son should not be taken to school any more. Thus, we are reminded, al-Mu'tasim remained unschooled and ignorant. One day a false prophet was arrested and brought before him.

'Are you a prophet?' asked the caliph.

The man answered in the affirmative.

'To whom has God sent you?'

'To you,' replied the man.

'You are indeed a stupid fool,' said the caliph.

'Wasn't it said that God chooses his prophets in the likeness of those who receive them?' said the man.

Thenceforth, the aliens, with their broken Arabic, weird manners, sadistic oppression, penny-pinching calculations and miserliness, lack of hospitality and ill-informed judgements, became the habitual targets of the wits and comedians.

A typical xenophobic joke which went into circulation repeatedly against the foreign occupiers from the Ottomans to the Israelis is the one about the Turkish *wali* who was crying and repenting his former crimes. His friend asked him what he had done. 'I killed four men,' said he.

'Four men only?' enquired the friend.

'Four Turkish men. I am not counting the *fallaheen*.'

The elements of the alien, the militarist and the whimsical ruler combined in the person of Qaraqush, to give us one of the most memorable characters in the literature of Arab humour. Qaraqush was a Turkish general who served under Saladdin and acted as his deputy over the affairs of Egypt. 'Qaraqush's rule' has become a platitude in describing any whimsical rotten government in the Arab world. More and more jokes and anecdotes were woven around his name until a worthy collection was compiled by Ibn Mammati under the fantastical title of *Al-Fashush fi Hukm Qaraqush*(The Nonsensical in the Rule of Qaraqush). The following are a few samples:

– A soldier was brought before him for colliding with a seven-months pregnant woman, causing a miscarriage. Quraqush's sentence against the soldier was that he should go and sleep with the said woman until she was seven months pregnant.

– The peasantry applied to him for an exemption from taxes because of the exceptionally cold weather which had killed their cotton plants. Application was rejected, for had the peasants taken the reasonable precaution of adding wool to the cotton, the cold wouldn't have killed the plants.

– A man in a coffin was crying and protesting as a multitude of people were taking him to be buried alive. Seeing Qaraqush passing by, he appealed to him. 'What?' said the governor, 'You want me to believe you and disbelieve the hundred mourners walking behind you?'

– A blacksmith killed a man and Qaraqush duly ordered his execution, but the local people made strong representation on his behalf claiming that he was a very useful tradesman for the community. Qaraqush sympathized with them and looked towards the door pensively until he saw a cage-maker passing by. 'All right. Execute him – the cage-maker! He is not useful.'

Another version of the last joke was also circulated in Europe and Freud discussed it in his book on jokes. Altogether, the character of Qaraqush emerged among other Middle Eastern nationalities, sometimes under different names, like Artin in Armenia. The Arabs mobilized their literary talents in their nationalistic fight against the Ajam (non-Arabs) and many of the distinguished poets and writers joined in this battle directly or indirectly. Al-Jahiz, for example, used his *Book of Misers* as a vehicle to get at the Persians. With their long traditions of hospitality, generosity and of being spendthrift, the Arabs looked at meanness and lack of hospitality as some of the most abominable traits in a man. Al-Jahiz, who wrote a great deal in defence of the supreme qualities of his people, used the opportunity of his book to spotlight this abomination in the Khurasanis, and the inhabitants of Maru in particular, and describe them as the meanest people in the world. In Khurasan, he wrote, your host asks you, 'Have you had your dinner?' If you replied in the affirmative he would say, 'If only you hadn't, I would invite you for a very delicious meal.' If you replied in the negative, he would say, 'If only you had, I would offer you five glasses of drink.' The most vile trait of the Khurasanis, he found, was their reluctance to entertain or eat together. 'The natural state for man,' said one of them, 'is to eat by himself and eating together is but an unnatural affectation.' But al-Jahiz found them quite willing to join together and share in one saucepan when it served their purpose:

> When they buy meat, they divide it before cooking and each of them ties his share to a string and puts it in the sauce and spices. Once cooked, each of them draws out his meat by pulling the carefully marked string. After that, they divide the gravy. When all the meat is eaten, piece by piece, they gather the strings and keep them. Should they decide to repeat the joint cooking, they use the same strings as they are well enriched with fat and gravy. Their participation is not for their desire for companionship, but because none of them is willing to bear all the cost of cooking for himself. Thus, they reduce the expense of the fire, vinegar, spices and garlic . . .

In another anecdote, al-Jahiz mentions that a group of Khurasanis decided to lighten the darkness of their nights by sharing an oil lamp, but one of them refused to pay his share of the cost and expense of the oil and wick. The impasse was happily resolved by blindfolding him every time they lit up the oil lamp and then releasing his eyes as soon as they put out the lamp and went to bed!

Of course, the Shu'ubids (the anti-Arab) did not keep silent and countered the Arab propaganda with their own, by ridiculing the nomadic and coarse habits of the Bedouins and, in the field of literature, the customary poetic tradition of 'crying over the remnants' (*al-buka' ala al-atlal*) with which the poet starts his *qasida* by recalling his departed love and describing the remnants of the desert encampment where once they were together and time was green and lush. Abu Nu'as, profligate humourist and Shu'ubid poet, ridiculed the typical names often mentioned in such poetry:

Who are Tamim, Qays and all their kin?
The Arabs in God's sight are nobody.

The Arabs, of course, always took great pride in their poetry. One of them said to a Persian, 'You have no poets among your people, and those few poets you have must be the sons of Arabs who slept with your women.' The Persian replied, 'And all those who are not poets among your people must be the sons of Persians who slept with Arab women.'

The inter-communal contest was partly an extension of the old tribal rivalry which had inspired gems of satirical poetry, and gained a climax in the famous verbal duels between Jarir (d. 728) and Farazdaq (d.728). In one of his famous pieces, Jarir used the same theme of stinginess to lash out at the tribe of Bani Taghlib:

A people who speak in whispers once they begin eating
And firmly bolt their gates and doors.
When a couple of guests arouse their dog's barking,
They call on their mother to piss on the fire.
Yet, too mean to give that, she witholds her urine
And passes it for them only by measures.

The devastating effect of satire may be assessed from the story given in *Kitab al-Aghani*. A poet of a lesser stature, Ra'i al-Ibil, of the tribe of Numayr, was riding his mule with his son, Jandal, and met Jarir. Jandal said to his father, 'Why do you halt before this dog of Bani Kulayb as though you had anything to hope or fear from him?' He gave the mule a lash which startled the animal and made him kick Jarir to the ground. Jarir got up, brushed his cap and recited:

O, Jandal, what will say Numayr of you
When my dishonouring shaft has pierced thy sire?

This he metaphorically did right through the night which he spent composing a satire of eighty verses against the Bani Numayr. At daybreak, he rode to where he could find Ra'i al-Ibil and Farazdaq with a group of people. With heads bowed down, they listened to the poet reciting. As soon as Jarir finished his last line, 'Cast down thine eyes for shame for thou art of Numayr,' Ra'i al-Ibil hurried to the people shouting, 'Saddle, saddle, you cannot stay here any longer.' They left Basra to rejoin the desert, with the whole tribe blaming Ra'i al-Ibil for the unnecessary ignominy which he brought upon it. For hundreds of years, we are told, Jarir's verses were quoted against Numayr.

With the decline of caliphate and loss of the religious aura of the ruler, the poets were released from their shackles and began to enjoy themselves in the exercise of the cherished form of *hija'*(satire), producing some of the most caustic lines ever known in Arabic literature, like this one in which the Abbasid poet, Bashshar Ibn Burd, attacked the Caliph al-Mahdi:

> A Caliph who copulates with his aunts
> And plays with birdlime and the polo mallet.

The following are but samples of what was in current use. One poet attacked the caliph's ministers:

> Gangs playing with the state!
> They were its arses, now they are its faces.
> Sa'id, Sa'dan, Sa'ida and the rest.
> Glory to Allah, who exposed and disgraced our world.

In a similar vein, Abu al-Fath wrote:

> At the door of our sultan stand a gang,
> A balsam to the eyes of their enemies!
> They are humble enough but they have stolen
> Three quarters of their titles.

Another poet wrote:

> Oh what a state, wherein there is no place,
> For a decent man to earn a grain
> Pass on to God's curse!
> Your ruler's mother is but a whore.

Ibn Bassam wrote this obituary on the death of the Prince of the Believers:

> They said our caliph is dead.

I said we have a dog and its like for a successor.
When shall we have an evil worse than his,
It will then be time to mourn and miss him.

A similar obituary was written in memory of the Abbasid minister
al-Fadhl bin Marwan:

To hell may he go, he and his like!
What have we lost to regret in his death?
God keep you, no eyes cry with running tears
For al-Fadhl, except those of the profligates and the compelled.

The caliphs were frequently changing or executing their ministers,
but Ibn Muqla must have had a special talent for survival as he
remained the serving minister for three caliphs, a phenomenon
which aroused a few comments and a lot of rumours:

They said dismissal is ministers' menstruation.
Curse it as a wretched business!
But Minister Abu Ali,
A lady past the menopause.

The judges, of course, received their full desserts from the poets,
especially in the Egypt of the Mamluk era when the *qadis* were
outbidding each other in corruption and purchasing their positions.
In this era, the poets seem to have lost all patience with the alien
Turkish authorities and thrown out of the window all restraint and
decorum. This opened the gate for the use of the vernacular and the
rise of the Halamantishi poetry, a kind of poetry of the absurd and
the ironical. Among the numerous anthologies is *Bada'i' al-Zuhur*
(The Splendour of Flowers) by Ibn Ayas, who included the following
verses about Ibn al-Naqib, the Chief Justice, who bought his position
by paying the sultan five thousand dinars and thus displaced al-
Qalqashandi who had paid only three thousand dinars. The
anonymous poets praised Ibn al-Naqib with these lines:

A qadi who, when two parties part in peace,
Rekindles their dispute with binding words.
Indifferent to this world and its luxuries, he seems,
But in secret, he wouldn't say no to a camel's dung.

Oh, people pause and hark

To the charming qualities of our *qadi*,
A homosexual, drunkard, fornicator, and takes bribes,
A tell-tale liar whose judgements follow his whims.

Like al-Mansur, the Ayubi ruler of Egypt, al-Malik al-Adil (the Just King) was tight-fisted, especially when dealing with the litterateurs, who reciprocated with this mean verse by Ibn Unayn:

Our hope, our Sultan
Rich in funds, short in spending.
He is a sword, as it is said,
But drawn to slash stipends and sustenance.

However, the most famous satirical poems in Arabic literature were composed by the all-time prince of Arabic poetry, Abu al-Tayyib al-Mutanabbi (915–65) in his virulent attack on Kafur al-Ikhshidi, the ruler of Egypt. Ambitious, self-centred, proud of his Arab lineage and education, one time a claimant to prophesy, al-Mutanabbi was reduced by fate and other people's jealousy to a beggar at the court of Kafur, a mere freed slave and usurper of office. The Mamluk ruler did not grant him his wishes and the poet had to escape from Cairo and write, under the stress of personal disgust and distress the two famous *qasidas* loaded with the typical racism of the Middle Ages. Moved by the emotions of the Day of Arafat (the eve of the Pilgrimage Feast) during his flight, he wrote:

In cash and treasures, I am the most carefree, rich man,
    For I am wealthy and my wealth is in promises.
I have settled with liars as their guest,
    Yet denied both hospitality and departure.
Men's generosity is through their hands, but theirs with
        tongues
    Oh that they and theirs were not.
Death doesn't take one of their souls
    Unless his hand had a trace of its stink.
With loosened belt, the flabby belly breaks wind,
    Neither counted among men nor yet among women.[6]
How is it that every time an evil slave kills his master
    Or betrays him, he finds advancement in Egypt?
There, the eunuch became leader of runaway slaves,
    The free is enslaved and the slave is worshipped.
Egypt's overseers have slept and let the foxes

Eat so much and still there are more grapes to eat.
Slaves are no brothers to goodly freeborn men,
        Even if born in the clothes of the free.
Never buy a slave without a stick,
        For slaves are filthy and evil.
I never thought I would live to a time
        When a dog would do me dirt and be praised,
Nor did imagine that no men would be found
        And that such son of the 'white' would do,[7]
And that this black man with his pierced camel lips,
        Would have trembling sycophants to rule.
Hungry, he eats from my food and detains me,
        So that he may be called a sought after potentate.
Men ordered about by a pot belly, woman-like slave
        Are indeed pathetic, aggrieved and enfeebled.
Curse it of a thought! Curse him who accepts it!
        For its like, the Mahri camels are born.
Faced with it, the taste of death is enjoyed,
        For death is sweat when one is humiliated.
Who taught the black eunuch any virtue,
        His nobel white people or his royal fathers,
Or his ear bleeding in the hand of the slave trader,
        Or his value of two pennies and yet rejected?
Little Kafur is the first to be excused
        Of all his villainy, and some excuses are damnations.
With the super white men lacking in goodness,
        How can we blame the black eunuchs?

In another poem in which the poet described his flight across
Sinai, he wrote verses which have become as famous and quotable
about the servility of the Egyptians as Hajjaj's words about the
rebelliousness of the Iraqis. But before launching his virulent attack
on Kafur's abject origin, he sets the standard by contrasting and
projecting his own nobility and high breeding:

When we made our camels kneel, we hoisted our spears,
        Over our virtues and our eminence
And spent the night kissing our swords
        And wiping them of our enemies' blood.
Let Egypt know and those in Iraq
        And those in al-Awasim that I am the youth,
That I have kept my word and resisted,

And treated with violence those who have been violent
Not everyone who gives his word fulfils,
    Nor anyone who suffers injustice rebels,
For the heart must have some tool
    And some belief that splits the hardest rock.
And he who has a heart like mine
    Splits the heart of destruction to reach glory.
And every youth who takes a path
    Makes his steps by the measure of his legs.
The little batman slept in our night,
    Having slept before in blindness not slumber.
Despite our proximity, there were between us
    Deserts of his ignorance and blindness.
I used to think before meeting this eunuch
    That the head was the place of reason,
But when I looked at his wits I saw
    That reason is altogether in the testicles.
What laughing stock in Egypt!
    But it is a laughter closer to weeping.
There, a Nabataean from the land of the black
    Teaches genealogies of the people of Arabia.
And another with his lip half his size
    And they call him 'Oh, moon of the night!'
In poetry I praised the rhinoceros,
    At times verses, at times spells.
Thus it was no praise for him,
    Rather a satire on the human race.
Some people went astray with idols,
    But with a wind bag, oh, no.
The idols are silent and he is talkative,
    And when moved, he farts or drivels.
When one is ignorant of his worth,
    Others see in him what he does not see.

The Age of Decadence witnessed the impoverishment of the majority of the people and the rise of various organizations adopting beggary, thieving and swindling as their way of life. The stories of Maqamat al-Hamathani and Maqamat al-Hariri related the adventurous stories of such heroes in a humorous and entertaining style so richly decorated that any translation would be an affront to the original. Authors started to record many anecdotes which had become current among the people, giving vent to their feelings and

illustrating the typical function of humour. One man was complaining of his state to his friend and the friend consoled him thus:
'Have patience. If a man in this crowded bazaar turned his head to
the archway and shouted: "Hey, you, misery!" he wouldn't find one
man who did not answer his call with the words, "Yes, here I am"!'

In another anecdote, a doctor was asked by his patient, 'What is
the best time for me to eat?'

'If you are rich,' answered the doctor, 'Eat whenever you feel like
eating. If you are poor, eat whenever you find food.'

Another story given by al-Kutubi in *Hazal al-Layali* (Nocturnal
Humour) and quoted by Arab wits recently on the occasion of the
Palestine conflict and its fate, illustrates the despair and futility of
trying to redress wrong and injustice. Both justice and injustice
agreed to buy and share a donkey for a journey they were
undertaking. After riding for a whole hour, justice dismounted as
agreed to give injustice her turn, but when that turn finished
injustice refused to give way. The two started to argue until they
came across some travellers whom they decided to consult. After
hearing the case properly the arbitrators ruled, 'Justice is on the side
of justice and injustice has no right to claim.' But injustice refused to
accept that verdict and decided to appeal to the next batch of
travellers and then to the next until they finally reached their
destination, with justice walking and injustice riding.

Numerous anecdotes about the craftiness of the beggars and the
meanness of the rich filled volumes and became the stock in trade of
the comic entertainers. A beggar knocked at somebody's door and
was answered by the owner, 'Sorry, my wife is out,' said the man.

'I am not asking for sex. I am only asking for a piece of bread,' said
the beggar.

Another stingy man answered the continuous line of beggars
with, 'May God the Most High give you succour,' until he was tired
of the routine. 'All these beggars! When shall I see the end of them?'
he said in despair.

'But why are you so upset', said his daughter, 'since you are giving
them only words?'

The most famous wit of the Islamic world was undoubtedly Juha,
the wise fool, mentioned in the foregoing chapter. No measure of his
popularity could be better than the jealous contest between the
Arabs, Turks, Iranians and Kurds to claim him as one of their
compatriots. He is even given more than one name, as his jokes
appear in Turkish attributed to a certain Khawaja Nasrildin,
supposed to be a contemporary of Tamerlane, the Mongol conqueror,

and in Persian under the name of Mullah Nasrildin. Arab scholars, however, insist on tracing him back to the reign of al-Mansur and al-Mahdi, when a certain jester called Abu al-Ghusn Dajni Ibn Thabit from the tribe of Fazara was nicknamed Juha and was responsible for some of the jokes which appeared later on in Turkish and Persian. As a matter of fact, Ibn Nadim mentions in the *Fihrist* (tenth century) a collection of Juha's jokes under the title of *Kitab Nawadir Juha*.[8] This is an academic point but, for the purpose of the present work, it seems that Juha was one of those folkloric characters who expressed the feelings and thoughts of people over a large area sharing similar conditions and history. An Arab prototype might have existed indeed and was later credited with more articulate and topical jokes and antics by the different nationalities which embraced Islam. Whereas Arab sources gave the year 160 A.H. as the year of his death, the Turks updated his life to the time of Tamerlane in the eighth century A.H. (fourteenth century A.D.) As it was, and regardless of their origin, Juha's anecdotes became part of the oral and written folklore of the Arab world and were destined in more recent history to become sources of inspiration in the field of contemporary politics. My own copy of Juha is a tattered, second-hand copy which I found in a remote Moroccan village offered for sale by a street pedlar.

Sometimes, Juha played the fool and feigned a Svejk-like stupidity in the face of a grim ruler, as when he was taken to meet Abu Muslim al-Khurasani, the ruthless architect of the Abbasid revolt against the Umayyads. Yaqtin, Abu Muslim's secretary, told him of his master's desire to see him. Juha responded and entered their office where he saw Abu Muslim and Yaqtin sitting waiting for him.

'O Yaqtin,' said Juha, 'Which of you is Abu Muslim?'

On other occasions, he appears cheeky and clever as when he was accompanying the *wali* to the bath and was asked by the *wali* with nothing on other than his towel, what he was worth.

'Fifty dinars', said Juha.

'Damn you, only my towel is worth fifty dinars,' remonstrated the *wali*.

'This is just what I allowed for,' replied Juha.

The frailties of the common folk are demonstrated by another type of anecdote reflecting the litterateurs' despair of and disdain for the masses. Tamerlane brought an elephant as a pet and the elephant spread havoc and disaster among the local people, treading on their crops, eating their produce, knocking down their stalls and carts, until they decided to send a delegation headed by Juha to speak to their ruler. A date was fixed for the meeting but as the delegation moved closer to the tyrant's palace, its members started to melt away until Juha found himself alone at the gate of the great hall.

'Well, what of my elephant?' enquired the Mongols' fearsome ruler.

'O, most illustrious Prince, the people have authorized me to tell you how happy they are with this elephant and how much pleasure he is giving them. Their only wish is to beg of you that you may complete their happiness and make this lovely elephant feel really at home by providing him with a female, so that they may breed and increase.'

On his way back, Juha saw the cowardly people. 'You were not satisfied with one elephant, now you will have two,' he told them.

In another episode Juha shared the mob instinct when he saw a crowd of people beating up a man, whereupon he hurried forthwith to join them in the beating.

'What are you beating him for?' enquired a passer-by.

'I don't know,' said Juha, 'I saw them beating him and joined them in expectation of God's reward.'

There are obvious discrepancies in the characterization of Juha and his attitudes which indicate different sources and different pens, but despite these differences, a general picture emerges of a religious man, wearing the turban of *faqih* (theologian), going about his business peacefully and honestly, inseparable from his donkey, hustled by his shrewish wife, rattled by the tyrannical whims of the ruler and exasperated with the frailties of the people. There is a cynical note in most of his words and actions, mingling with the endemic sadness and fatalism of the Middle East. Hearing of a job to teach speech to the donkey of the prince, he went forward and offered his services. 'I accept the condition,' he said to the prince, 'that you may execute me if I fail in my undertaking. Only I need twenty -five years to do the job.'

The prince agreed and the deal was clinched. Back at home, his wife started her harangue as usual. 'You fool, how can you teach an ass to speak?'

Juha answered: 'In twenty-five years, either the prince dies, the donkey dies or I myself die.'

I was reminded of this story and the lasting impression which Juha has made on the people of the Middle East when I read the manuscript of a novel satirizing an Arab head of state. 'Surely you can't publish that! They will crucify you,' I said to the author.

'Don't worry. By the time I find a publisher and the book goes to press, either I die, our president is toppled or my publisher goes bust.'

The heavy hand of tyranny fell most heavily on the Middle East during the rein of Tamerlane, and many of Juha's anecdotes refer to the government of this Mongol ruler. One day, he decided to check the books of one of his governors. After finding some flaws in his accounts which Tamerlane did not like, he ordered the governor to eat all his books on pain of death, and then he appointed Juha as an auditor. When the next year expired and the time of reckoning arrived, Juha brought with him the year's accounts written on bundles of unleavened bread.

Almost every Juha joke is an example of humour as a rectifier of a social imbalance and misdemeanour. Many are boringly didactic and a few share the same path followed by other humourists in exposing the corruption and ignorance of the *qadis* and rulers. As time passed with the Arab peoples writhing under the decadent administration of the Ottomans, more and more of such jokes and anecdotes were invented and circulated to create a whole body of oral literature passing from mouth to mouth in the bazaars and cafes, and occasionally voiced by mob demonstrations in the streets. Al-Jabarti gave details of the people's chants and slang verses, often biting in their sarcasm and ridicule, as in al-Sharbini's poem *Haz al-Quhuf fi Sharh Qasidat Abi Shaduf* (Shaking the Fragments in Explaining Abu Shaduf's poem) which held a humorous mirror to the sad conditions of the peasantry and appealed for their amelioration. Of course, most of the topical jokes had been lost, but many of them were still current when the dawn of Arab revival broke in the beginning of the nineteenth century, with the added ingredients of European culture and sense of humour – but this is the subject of the next chapter.

الموقف السياسى !!

— يجب أن لا نتعاون مع الجماعة المستقلين
لأن غرضهم يستفيدوا على حسابنا !

— مالناش دعوة بأحزاب المعارضة لان
غرضهم يستفيدوا على حسابنا احنا يامستقلين

— لازم نبعد مكرم باشا من وسطنا لان مكرم
كل غرضه يستفيد على حسابنا !

'The Political Situation', Sarukhan, *Akhir Sa'a* 1944. The captions
read, left to right:

'We must not cooperate with the independents because their aim is
to benefit at our expense';

'We should have nothing to do with the opposition parties because
they want to benefit at our expense';

'Our duty is to keep Mukarram Pasha out because all he wants is to
benefit at our expense'.

3 The Age of Resurgence: the Satirical Press

> There is another way of dealing with the excessively humorous newspapers and that is by answering their humour with humour and their trifling with trifling.
>
> Taha Hussein

The Middle East was rudely shaken from its slumber in 1798, when Napoleon invaded Egypt and started a process of infinite dimensions, in which the legacy and provisions of the past were contrasted so unfavourably with the equipment, both mental and technical, of Europe. In 1922, Amin al-Rayhani expressed this feeling with a much quoted passage, 'I am the Orient... I have philosophies; I have religions. Is there anyone who might buy them from me for aircraft?' In his attempt to catch up with the West, Muhammad Ali the Great, the new ruler of Egypt, enhanced this process by sending many missions to study in France and translating the works of the Europeans into Arabic. The Abbasids had translated the knowledge of the Greeks, but that was a dead and remote culture, especially where literature was concerned. Modern European literature was a living thing and enjoyed a more universal and immediate appeal. The literate Arabs must have been stunned by the profound magic of the great European masterpieces of arts and literature. I can draw only on my own personal experience to imagine that impact. As soon as I read Bernard Shaw's *St Joan* and Darwin's theory of evolution in my early teens, all the old prose of Arabic literature receded for me into nothing and the only pressing task I could see ahead of me was to master a European language as soon as possible. This impression was even more fortified by my teacher, Jasim Muhammad al-Rijab, who urged all students to learn English with the words, 'Two paragraphs in English are worth an entire Arabic bookshop.' The funny side of his advice was the fact that he was our teacher of Arabic literature! It took us years before we could restore some balance to our view and regain faith in our national heritage.

Under this impact, Arab writers went into a book shoplifting spree, translating, adapting, vandalizing, pirating, readapting and rehashing anything falling into their hands. As mentioned before, the Arabs have a great predilection for fun, but despite their prodigious production in this field, their range and variety were limited. Parallel with the adoption of Europe's technical inventions went the adoption of its artistic creativeness, and the first obvious borrowing was the art of comedy. The earliest translations in this field appeared in Syria when Salim al-Naqqash and Adib Ishaq translated Molière's *L'Avare* and *Tartuffe*, but the first native excursion in dramatic satire was made in Cairo in 1872 by the versatile Ya'qub Sannu'. It is most important to recall and note with care the life of this political agitator. Sannu' was the son of an Egyptian Jewish mother and an Italian father, but on account of some superstitious belief, his mother made an oath to bring him up in the Islamic faith, and young Ya'qub had all the education and discipline of a good Muslim but, with his parental background, he also made sufficient effort to learn Hebrew and study the Old and New Testaments. At the age of twelve, he was reading the Qur'an in Arabic, the Old Testament in Hebrew and the New Testament in English,[1] and finished his education in Italy, whose language, together with French, he had already mastered. Sannu' studied both painting and music and taught both subjects in schools. He spent the second part of his life in exile in France, married a Catholic and had children who grew up in Europe as Christians. No man could be more cosmopolitan and no Egyptian had better first-hand access to European culture and thought.

Long before this history, folk artists satirized, in shadow plays and mimicry, the overbearance of the rich, the foreigner and the powerful, but Sunnu' turned to the more legitimate theatre by organizing a dramatic company from a makeshift theatre, for which he wrote his own plays denouncing in comic terms the evils of his society. Many 'firsts' in the history of Arabic comedy and humour may be traced back to this man, and one of his firsts was his indictment of polygamy in his play *The Two Wives*, which naturally aroused the anger of the traditional and clerical. The khedive, who had enjoyed his other plays and honoured him with the title of 'Egypt's Molière', called him to the palace and warned him against such encroachment on religion and tradition. 'If your balls,' said the notorious womaniser khedive, 'cannot satisfy more than one woman, do not expect others to be like you.'[2] Another first was his satire on British imperialism in his play *The Tourist and the*

Donkey which caricatured John Bull and prompted the British to denounce him to the khedive as a dangerous person. The theatre, and with it the first chapter of Arabic drama, was closed by order a few months later and its founder turned to another field. Ya'qub Sannu' was a disciple of the agitator and reformer, Jamal al-Din al-Afghani who, realizing the value of humour in the political arena, urged the young writer to start a satirical newspaper, which he then launched in 1877 with the title of *Abu Naddara Zarqa* (The Man with the Blue Spectacles), a publication dedicated to humour 'without ever involving itself in religion or national politics', a promise which was hardly kept. Realizing the constraints in dealing with the khedive, the establishment and the British, he resorted to the familiar Arab method of discussing the past and relating old but relevant anecdotes, as he did in 'The Rule of Qaraqush'. His tales were frequently given in the form of a dialogue between the two characters of Abu Khalil and Abu Naddara. With a typical tongue-in-the-cheek piece, he defended the corrupt and despotic Khedive Ismael in what is known in Arabic literature as *Al-tham min bab al madh* (dispraise in the way of praise).

Abu Khalil: What is so frivolous about this paper, sir? What's in it is most serious and the government should be pleased with it. It shows the people the kind of injustice which they suffered in the days of the *Ghaz* and the justice and fairness which is prevailing now in the era of our Egypt's King, the meek, the compassionate, the one who loves his subjects like his own dear children, as you see.

Abu Naddara: Yet, some *amirs* do not understand this. God will bring out the truth.

If no other people managed to grasp the truth, the khedive did, and he unleashed his henchmen to ambush Sannu' but the hunted editor survived his injury and lived to fight more battles. Rumour had it that the khedive was killing his enemies by poisoning their coffee and Sannu' was warned against it. Abu Khalil and Abu Naddara had something to say about it as they were being entertained:

– What would you like to have?
– Abu Naddara is a martyr to beer.
– Perhaps the man would like to have some coffee.

Abu Naddara: Oh, no brother. I don't like coffee these days. It has become dangerous and the man who drinks just one cup of coffee will snuff it.

Sannu' was eventually exiled to France where he launched a series of newspapers with different names revolving around what had become his trade mark, '*Abu Naddara Zarqa*'. He used different ways in smuggling his publications to Egypt. In Alexandria, the British governor of the city, a Mr Orfry, could do nothing but contract the local clandestine newsagent to sell him every consignment of the five hundred copies arriving from Paris, which Mr Orfry then destroyed. When Sannu' – who was in terrible financial straits – heard of the story, he hastened to send an additional five hundred copies to his agent for the normal sale to the anxious customers. For months to come, the British governor went on unwittingly subsidizing the subversive newspaper. Quite a joke on its own!

From his exile he went on lashing out at his former master (Sannu' was the teacher of the royal princes).

> It is sufficient to say that he recognizes not one good and rejects not one sin. At prayer time, you find him unclean for prayer, and in Ramadan unobservant of fasting. Aye, he does fast but from all good work, and welcomes sinfulness soiled with the filth of fornication, a debauchee who thrives on cardinal sins and amuses himself with the lesser evils. To God, he turns grumbling and to the devil he bows in gratitude. He looks like one who has pledged himself to Satan and has never broken his pledge, and promised him every single sin without ever failing in his promise. When pious and good people are mentioned, he calls, 'Bring me my physician,' and when the evil and wicked are mentioned, he says, 'Oh, sing me their praise.'

His second, or rather first target after Khedive Ismael, was the British, whom he hated – both as an Egyptian patriot and as a Francophile. When the Sudan took up arms against the British forces in August 1888 he hailed its initial success in his article, 'The Tower of Eiffel', in which he said that from the top of the famous tower (symbol of France), he could see 'the lions of the Sudan treating the British with their spears like pig kebab meat moulded on skewers, moistened with donkey's urine'. Sannu' was resolved never to set foot again on Egyptian soil as long as the British were there. When Lord Cromer retired from office as lord and master of Egypt in 1907 and Sannu' was urged to return to Cairo, he wrote about the Roman despot who was surprised to see a woman, on his way to war, praying to the gods that he might return safe and victorious. He, therefore, interrogated her on the matter and she gave him this answer: Your father was a tyrant and when he died he gave us a worse tyrant in you. I fear that if you die, we may have someone still worse than you. 'I am not going to rejoice at the departure,' Sannu' commented, 'until I see the one who is coming next.'³

Despite the many firsts which Sannu' had introduced in the Arab political arena, he himself was not an original thinker or a great intellect, and the foregoing citations sum up the depth and width of his wit, due allowances to the loss of the original Arabic nuances and rhymes being made. His ideas were those of contemporary westernized society, but his style was still in the traditional mould based on lampoon, saj' (a kind of rhymed prose which can be quite effective in Arabic), zajal (a form of vernacular poem), crude swearing and slander, resort to moral fables and historical episodes and mockery of the broken Arabic of the foreigners. Like many humorous writers, he used the vernacular for comic effect, assuming that the mere elevation of common speech to the respectability of print is sufficient cause for laughter. His artistic training helped him to introduce the art of the caricature to Arabic journalism but, as can be seen from the illustrations, his drawings remained primitive and tentative, but not always without a clever idea. Among his notable caricatures made during his exile was one about Khedive Ismael (the ruler who burdened Egypt with debts) shown as a news vendor selling in the street Egypt's leading daily, *Al-Ahram*. In Arabic *Al-Ahram* means 'the pyramids', the symbol of Egypt, and the newspaper bears a little drawing of the pyramids on top of the title. Sannu's hint is obvious.

The next character we meet in this field of political agitation is Abdullah al-Nadim, who combined the religious training of a shaykh with the revolutionary fervour of a socialist and the satirical humour of a *zarif* and street entertainer. Like Ash'ab and Juha, he became a popular legend around which many jokes and anecdotes were woven. He was born of a poor proletarian family and worked as a servant in the villa of a rich aristocrat. At a very early age he showed his predilection for satire and rebellion when he composed a piece of *zajal* mocking the lady of the house, for which he was beaten up with clogs until he was unconscious.

In his more mature years, he was credited with the publication of *Al-Tankit wa Al-Tabkit* (Joking and Censure), a humorous newspaper which appeared in June 1887 revealing a promising talent. The themes were mainly social, like the one about the westernized native boy who spent his childhood playing with mud, sleeping on the village garbage and driving the cattle like one of them, until he was sent by the government to study in Europe. This is a theme which comes up time and time again in Arabic comedy. The young boy with the comic name of Zi'it returns from Europe to the embrace of his father with the comic rhyming name of Mi'it.

Zi'it: You Muslims, have this very awful habit of embracing!

Mi'it: Then, my son, how do we greet each other?

Zi'it: Say *'Bon arrivée'* and put your hand into mine once, and that's the end of it.

Mi'it: I do say, me son, I'm not no villager.

Zi'it: Not a villager! O, you *shaykh*, you Arabs are like animals.

The mother serves dinner and the son finds the food too hot for his new taste. Why have you put too much of ... What do you call it? The village boy has forgotten the name of pepper ... and of garlic, onions, wheat, etc.

In later years, a story was circulated in Syria about a graduate from the Sorbonne who returned to his homeland and stood in feigned bewilderment in front of a palm tree. 'Oh, what is this tall thing?'

Interesting to note that al-Nadim was giving his stories and articles the form of a dialogue, showing already the impact of Western dramatic technique, as in the following piece exposing the exploitation of the *fallaheen* (peasantry) by the money lenders:

– I've come for a loan at interest, sir.

– The interest is twenty per cent per annum.

– Do what you think right.

– Take twenty from the hundred, how much is left?

– I can neither read nor write. You see how much is left.

– The balance is seventy.

– Ah, just about.

– There. Now you owe me a hundred. Add twenty, and write the IOU note.

– You write and here is my seal.

For a whole year, the *fallah* goes on delivering wheat, cotton, beans and barley to the usurer and then visits him to settle.

– Sir, show me my accounts.

– You delivered cotton for twenty pounds, wheat for twenty pounds and barley for ten pounds. How much is that?

– I told you last time. I can't do sums.

– Well, they make forty. Take that from the hundred and twenty. How much is left?

– Who ever knows what's beyond that!

– The balance is ninety. The interest on it is twenty. That makes it 115. You want another loan of thirty. That makes it 160. Add to it forty pounds interest and that brings us to 210½ pounds for which you have to write me a new IOU note.

– What's that? There were seven tens in origin, then two more tens and add to that thirty-three. You take from them the price of the things I delivered to you. The balance is 210 only. Where did you get the half?

– This is the charge of my writing the IOU note.

In his article 'The Soirée of Fun', we meet a sensible patriot who comes across a typical group of revellers, 'with one hanging his head over his shoulders, another resting on a pillow, a third swaying like a sleepwalker, another man with his hands on his cheeks'. He ventured to ask them what grave subject they were discussing. Would it be the trade or rising wealth and might of Europe and the press reports on the affairs of the world?

'What have we got to do with Europe and its people? We haven't left Egypt in all our lives . . . History is something for the scientist and newspapers are only read by the *khawajas* [foreigners].'

The guest tries to arouse their sense of national duty. 'Oh, this is something which gives us a headache and distracts the mind. Only those who have nothing else to do meddle with it . . Whether the country goes forward or backward, it won't bring us anything better.'

'What has brought you together then?' asks the guest. 'It is the custom of fun. Man can only be happy when he sits in a gathering of amusement and laughter and play. We meet to entertain each other and crack jokes among ourselves until we begin to hum and feel numb and go to sleep.'

The revellers join in one refrain. 'What have we got with the world and its economy or history. Do you want us to become like the *khawajas* who stop every hour and check what has been happening on earth and what the papers have said and the cables reported like people who own the world?'

In another, somewhat peculiar article, under the heading of 'Man's Injustice in Calling the Animals Savages', al-Nadim tackled the unusual theme of man's aggression on animals and expressed distinct naturalistic influences. Some animals, he wrote, looked upon human society and felt revulsion against its squalid civilization, iniquity, claustrophobia and artificiality, and decided to keep away from it. They did not like this aggressive and murderous creature called man, but for their refusal to be domesticated into his service, he called them savage beasts and gave himself licence to hunt them and kill them.

Oh man! How good was your origin, the beauty of your image, the dignity of your personality, the wealth of your science and the excellence of your mind! Oh you of the sublime origin, how ugly

are you now with your excessive pride, with your boast over your
silly compositions and with your aggrandizement and false
imagination that you are the only one in the universe.

Egypt was soon moved to take up arms against the British in what
is known as the Arabi Revolt. The day had come for al-Nadim to
throw in his lot with the patriots and use his power of oratory to
agitate the people to rise and fight the foreign occupiers of the
country. After the collapse of the revolt, he disappeared and went on
roaming, incognito, the towns and villages relating, in cafes, the
jokes of the man called Abdullah al-Nadim, long ceased to be among
the living. 'May Allah have mercy upon the soul of al-Nadim,' his
listeners used to murmur. Worried about what the authorities
might do to them, his servant thought of delivering him to the
police, and the two spent their time watching each other, until one
day al-Nadim decided to put an end to it. He suddenly threw down
the newspaper, saying, 'Oh, there is no power or means except
Allah's. The government is offering a reward of a thousand pounds
to whoever guides them to me, and five thousand pounds to the man
who guides them to my servant.' With that, the servant became even
more concerned about their disguise than the master, and al-Nadim,
in his human nature, rewarded the servant for this practical joke by
the only thing he could give – teaching him reading and writing.
Hunted by the authorities, weakened by poverty, Abdullah al-
Nadim died of tuberculosis – hardly noticed by anyone.
   At that time and until the overthrow of King Farouk, the old
burden of foreign rule was even more compounded as the ruling
family was Albanian, the power was in the hands of the British, the
nominal title belonged to the Turks and all the economic structure
and businesses were in the hands of Greeks, Italians, French, etc.
The Egyptian was made a stranger in his own town. Many Arabs
who visited Cairo's top restaurants, in the old days, were appalled
when they discovered that no one served them if they spoke in
Arabic. The worst feature of this state was the existence of the
Mixed Courts, which included judges from the foreign powers and
had the authority of superseding all courts in Egypt in any case
involving a foreigner. The Islamic or native justice was considered
not good enough for a European, and the Egyptians often abandoned
their case as soon as it was referred to the Mixed Court. The *khawaja*
(foreigner) became a complex with the natives who could find no
answer to it other than the old weapon of humour. Like many others,
al-Nadim enlarged on it. Thus, he reported that one day a policeman

saw a burglar descending with a bundle of loot from a window. The policeman shouted: 'Who is that?'

'A *khawaja*,' replied the burglar.

'Oh, pardon me . . .,' said the policeman, 'I thought you were an Egyptian.'

In the aftermath of the Arabi revolt and the massacre of many demonstrators, al-Nadim was seen amid the fallen, examining the corpses. 'What are you doing?' someone asked him.

'Just to assure myself that they are really dead. After all, the Angel of Death may be a *khawaja*.'

Abdullah al-Nadim's wrath was not directed against the *khawajas* only, but also against his own submissive people who accepted their lot so meekly. During the anti-British demonstrations, he vented his feelings against the Egyptians as much as against the British *khawajas*. 'Oh, people of Egypt, smell your bodies. They are stinking dirty whilst the Nile is flowing in your midst. Listen to your cries of woe whilst your valley is full of goodness. Listen to the voice of God as he curses you whilst you learn his book by heart and carry his message.'[4]

Another satirical magazine issued in Egypt was *Misbah al-Sharq* (The Light of the East) published and edited by Ibrahim al-Muwaylihi, a writer known for his direct, sharp and brutal satire. A compilation of his articles appeared later on under the heading of 'What is There', which included his thirteen hilarious dispatches from Istanbul, the seat of the Ottoman Caliphate. The Saray (government house) included the offices of the chief of protocol, the chief clerk, the chief *agha* and the chief spy. The latter's post, however, was later abolished as all chiefs were made responsible for spying, with informers in every department. In another dispatch, al-Muwaylihi described the life and functions of the courtiers: 'There is no word in any language', he wrote, 'which can express singularly all the evils collectively as the word "courtier" . . . The word imparts the three characteristics of marble: heavy, cold and smooth, just like a tombstone. Thus kings may surround themselves with these qualities both in life and in death.'

During his stay in Istanbul, France invaded Tunisia and the liberal Madhat Pasha escaped from the clutches of the chief spy and sought asylum in the French consulate. After long diplomatic notes and negotiations, the two empires agreed that France deliver the rebel to Turkey and Turkey concede the whole of Tunisia to France. 'Thus,' he wrote, 'Turkey has bought one man for the price of a whole kingdom and showed how much value she sets on human beings.' Commenting on the practice of exiling politicians and courtiers to Mecca, he wrote pointedly that the sultan 'vents his displeasure by sending them from the house of the sultan to the house of the *Rihman* (God)'.

In his article 'The Spies', he said that in other countries men usually attained their ascendance by learning, heroic combat and overcoming difficulties, but in Istanbul, the path is short. People attained wealth, glory and fame in one day – simply by fabricating a charge against some innocent man. The sultan accustomed himself to listen every morning to a report from his spies about some plot against his person. If no such report reached him, he would then worry himself and assume that the worst had happened and the conspirators had outwitted his spies. The sultan would then spend his hours in panic until he was rescued by his informers with a fabricated report about a conspiracy. Once that report was proved to be groundless, the sultan would then feel relieved and spend the rest of his day joyfully. Once, a courtier complained to him of the pressure of his work because he received reports about not less than three plots between one ablution and another. Al-Muwaylihi returned to the subject again in his ninth despatch by relating how a Syrian called on Munif Pasha offering what was called 'his slavery' in return for some menial appointment. It was believed that the sultan was used to invite his enemies to Yâldûz Palace, kill them and dump them into the Bosphorus. Munif Pasha asked his Syrian acquaintance for his address in Istanbul.

'The Yâldûz Palace,' the supplicant replied.

'How is that?' whispered the pasha.

'The hotel near Sarkaçi,' explained the man.

Munif Pasha jumped to his feet. 'Get up and don't sit here until you move to another hotel.'

The sultan was under the influence of Shaykh al-Islam, the religious leader who was always found by his side, playing on his susceptibility with myths and superstitions. They both believed in al-Khidr, the eternal prophet who roams the world unseen by anyone except the chosen few. One day, when they were both by themselves alone, Shaykh al-Islam turned his head abruptly and returned the salutation, 'And peace be upon you.' The amazed sultan looked at the shaykh and said, 'Whom did you greet?' The shaykh simply murmured, 'Oh, this was al-Khidr just passing by.'

The collection was published anonymously but the sultan's spies didn't fail in their duty this time and the Ottoman tyrant ordered the confiscation of all copies, but the author hastened to collect them and send them to him. The articles achieved great popularity but Muhammad Abduh, the famous religious reformer, was not given to excessive enthusiasm as the rest of his countrymen have been, and was used to understatement and modesty. Whenever the younger writer showed him an article which received enthusiastic acclaim, Muhammad Abduh simply nodded his head gently and said *mush battal* (not bad). In his frustration with his senior mentor, he wrote:

> If the God of the Universe sat on his throne on the Day of Judgement surrounded by his favourite angels and flanked on his right by his prophets and messengers and followed at the back by all the varieties of genies, devils, birds and beasts, and then someone asked Muhammad Abduh: 'What do you think of all this sight?' he would simply say, 'Not bad.'[5]

His next famous work is his book *Hadith Isa Ibn Hisham* with essays criticizing and satirizing Western civilization, or rather more specifically those who adopted the trappings of its ugly face, by now quite an established theme. Muhammad al-Muwailihi spent a great part of his life outside Egypt, which prompted him to coin the epigram that: 'Egypt is like a cemetery, a place to visit but not to inhabit.'

These pioneers paved the way for a series of humorous and satirical newspapers to appear in the early twentieth century, like *Khayal al-Zil* (Shadow Puppets) of Ahmad Hafiz Awad, *al-Sayf* (The Sword), *al-Masamir* (The Nails) and *al Sa'iqa* (The Thunderbolt). Just before the Great War, the same al-Muwailihi published two magazines after the names of the two old humorous personalities: Abu Nu'as and Abu Zayd. Abd al-Majid Kamil issued *al-Babaghlu al-Misri*, and Abd al-Hamid Zaki started *al-Siyasa al-Musawwara* (Pictorial Politics). Practically all these newspapers carried caricatures and *al-Lata'if al-Musawwara* (Pictorial Anecdotes) was distinguished by its two cartoonists, Nihad Khulusi, who was of Turkish origin, and Ihab. The development of this art was interrupted by the outbreak of hostilities in Europe and the entry of Turkey into the war. Censorship was declared and many of these troublesome magazines disappeared from the market. The end of the war, however, and the rise of the struggle for national independence produced the leading magazines which played an important role in Egyptian politics and occupied a lasting place in the history of Arabic journalism. In 1921 Sulayman Fawzi started *al-Kashkul*, which opposed the anti-British nationalist leader and founder of the

Wafd Party, Sa'ad Zaghlul, and in 1925, Mrs Rose al-Youssef started a
pro-Zaghlul magazine, the most famous humorous journal in the
Arab world, bearing her own name. In the long feud between the
Wafdists (supporters of Sa'ad Zaghlul) and al-Ahrar (the Constitutional Liberals), both magazines had an uneven history as they fell
in and out of favour in their support of the two political parties.
Al-Kashkul supported first the liberal leader, Muhammad Hussein
Haykal, but turned against him in the thirties and described him, on
23 January 1931, as an antiquarian using weird mysticism in his
writings as much as in politics. 'He is like a piece of dough or clay in
the hands of skilful artists using it to make statues, or like the disc of
a phonograph picking up haphazardly other people's voices and
obeying their directives.'

Among the various contributors to al-Kashkul was Hussein
Shafiq al-Misri, a writer with great sense of humour and wit, which
he used repeatedly, often in the poetic form of zajal, in ridiculing the
establishment and its application of the laws and regulations.
Among his inventions was the character of Sergeant Sha'la Abd
al-Maujud, another tool in Hussein's onslaught on the authorities,
the capitalist system and the exploitation of the people.

The most noteworthy phenomenon in this history is the close
connection between humour and the theatre, demonstrated by the
Arab world in support of Meredith's thesis on the subject (see
Chapter 1). The identification of the dramatist and the satirical
columnist in the person of the pioneering Ya'qub Sannu' repeated
itself in more than one crossroads in this history and in many Arab
countries. Behind the two lines of development, there was the more
basic and no less tentative development of democracy and
parliamentary life. Side by side with the appearance of the satirical
publications, there appeared numerous translations of European
plays and a string of theatrical companies including the George
Abyadh troupe which specialized in comedies and vaudeville, the
Zaki Tulaymat company which witnessed the rise of the star
comedian, Ali al-Kassar, and the Aziz Id Company. All the time,
comedians moved from the stage to the editorial desks, and writers
of humour moved from their desks to the stage. Rose al-Youssef was,
in fact, a successful actress of Lebanese origin and a contemporary of
Ya'qub Sannu'. Like him, she had a social conscience and was much
perturbed by the conditions of the country around her, and like him
also she had a multi-religious background, having been brought up
as a Muslim with the name of Fatima, become a convert to
Christianity and reverted to Islam in her later years. Multi-

fariousness in faith is one way, it seems, of making people conscious of the funny side of dogma. Her interest in public affairs and the national struggle for liberation in general, led her in the end to decide to quit the stage and start the magazine which bore her name and adopted her approach to political enlightenment through the typically Egyptian means of humour.

Rose al-Youssef became a school in this field and many of the great names in Arabic satirical journalism, like Fikri Abadha, Muhammad al-Tabi'i and Salah Thihni, received their initiation on the pages of this publication. Among the regular columnists of the period were Ali Shauki and Abd al-Warith Asir (soon to achieve great fame as an actor), who wrote the hilarious series of Abu Zi'ayzi' and Zi'ayzi', in verse and prose.

The inventiveness of the writers was more than matched by the skilful rendering of such renowned cartoonists as Alexander Sarukhan and Salah Jahin, who also wrote satirical verses; George al-Bahjuri, Abd al-Muním Rakha and al-Hijazi. The prototype characters which flowed from the pens of these cartoonists, like al-Misri Effendi (Mr Egyptian), Bint al-Balad (the daughter of the town), Ibn al-Balad (the son of the town) and Kishkish Bey became household names throughout the Arab world. Even more lasting in fame and humour were the eternal couple, Rafi'a Hanim (Lady Thinwoman – otherwise enormous and domineering) and al-Sab' Effendi (Mr Lionman – otherwise a mouse of a man, skinny, tiny and timid). The couple represented a furtive mockery on Mrs Nahhas Pasha and her husband, the Wafdist leader and Prime Minister, who was hen-pecked by his wife like many Egyptian politicians. Humar Effendi (Mr Donkey) was a caricature version of the old anthropomorphic tradition – a gentleman with the head of an ass and a pair of reading glasses. In one cartoon by Rakha, Nahhas Pasha points to the donkey: 'There is absolutely no similarity between me and him, except in the way we think.'

The extent of the popularity of these caricature characters may be demonstrated by the fact that only a few years after the invention of al-Misri Effendi in 1932 by Muhammad al-Tabi'i and Sarukhian, the name became the trade name of numerous stores, barbers' salons and even shoe-repair shops as well as the title of the leading weekly, *al-Misri Effendi*. With these cartoonists, the art of the caricature reached its maturity and began to make great impact on the politicians, so much so that Hussein Sirri Pasha felt very upset by the white hair which Sarukhan was giving him and invited the gifted artist to have a good look at his real black hair! Rakha, however, was less fortunate as his aggressive cartoons landed him in gaol for more than a year.

Naturally *Rose al-Youssef* was sensitive to any matter related to the theatre, and only a few months after its first issue (26 October 1925), the magazine crossed swords with the minister, Ahmad Bey Khashaba. In 1926, the hapless minister ventured, after a performance of *Antony and Cleopatra*, to go on stage and congratulate the actress. *Rose al-Youssef* carried the usual notice and added that a number of ministers attended the performance and one of them (without even identifying him at this stage) went and congratulated the cast. The security police circled the paragraph in red and referred it for action against the magazine. The following week, the magazine carried an article under the heading 'A Gross Error' saying:

> A gross error was committed when the minister forgot himself and his position at the time and condescended to demean himself by stretching his gracious hand to shake the contemptible hand of a male performer and a female singer. This was a great weakness from the minister and a terrible error which the press should cover up and conceal from the public, otherwise the minister may lose respect in their eyes.

After identifying the artists as Muhammad Abd al-Wahhab and Munira al-Mahdia (two famous Egyptian singers), the writer went on to make comparisons, mentioning that only a few weeks before, the Queen of England attended the last performance of Madame Melba, shook hands with her and presented her with flowers. 'If, however,' the article added, 'the officer at the Public Security considered that there is a great difference between Madame Melba and Munira al-Mahdia, I can assure him that there is also a great difference between the Queen of England, the Empress of India and Ahmad Bey Khashaba, the Minister of both our Army and Navy.' As it happens, no one knows in the Arab World now who Ahmad Bey Khashaba was or is. Everyone knows who Muhammad Abd al-Wahhab is and most Arab ministers do and *did* wish that they could shake hands with him.

The issue of *Rose al-Youssef* coincided with the great controversy over Taha Hussein's book, *Al-Shi'r al-Jahili* (Pre-Islamic Poetry), and the doubts which it cast on many of the sacred 'facts' connected with it, and the outcry that the writer was spreading atheism! The magazine picked up the gauntlet and asked: 'Is it part of Egypt's destiny that the minds of her sons and their right to express their opinions must remain subject to a handful of old men afflicted with gout and indigestion?'

Dealing with the widespread nepotism of the Middle East, *Rose al-Youssef* ridiculed the hypocrisy of the members of Parliament.

It is indeed very satisfying to see one of the honourable gentlemen stand up in the Chamber of Deputies and attack nepotism and its advocates, call for the cancellation of all appointments inspired by influence, and cause a problem which may require a vote of confidence. All this is good and splendid. But shouldn't such deputies feel ashamed of themselves that shortly before coming to the chamber and kicking up all this storm, they visited government departments and called on the top executives to use their influence in appointing Fulan, promoting Allan and yielding to Tartan?[6]

In this land ruled by old men suffering from gout, *Rose al-Youssef* carried the banner of progress, reform and liberation. When the Ministry of Education closed the Institute of Drama on the grounds that it was encouraging immorality and Taha Hussein was dismissed for allowing mixed education at the Faculty of Arts, the editor dropped the title of the Minister of Education and called him the Minister of Tradition. But soon the magazine invented new titles for all ministers. The Minister of Agriculture was called the Minister of Pests and Salinity, the Minister of Communications , who pestered everyone with his duodenal ulcer, was called the Minister of Intestines. The Ministry of Defence was rebaptized the Ministry of Adornments. The Ministry of Health was described as the Ministry for the Eradication of Illness by Putting Down All Ill People and the Ministry of Communications was described as the Ministry Cursed by Travellers Both Ways of the Journey. The Ministry of Religious Endowments was identified as the Ministry which Protected the Dead and Killed the Living; the Ministry of the Interior was the Ministry which Insured the Interests of Individuals and the Seats of Ministers; the Ministry of Justice prevented urban competition by throwing into prison the petty criminals. Mrs Rose al-Youssef would have very much liked to find a nickname for King Fu'ad as well, but that would have put her in clear defiance of the law which she could and did only avoid by publishing numerous articles about the past decadent and despotic monarchs who lost their heads, ended in prison and exile and incurred the curse of their people and of history.

The article about Charles I was even supported by pictures for good measure.

The magazine, of course, lost no opportunity in tackling the question of independence and the British rule. In 1927, another such opportunity presented itself in the visit of the British High Commissioner to Jiza. 'If His Excellency the High Commissioner visited the Ophthalmic Hospital in al-Jiza, why should the Provincial Governor, the Chief Constable and the Government Deputy gather to receive him? Why a police detachment to make a military salute? If the ambassador of France, Italy or Belgium visits the same hospital, will the Governor, the Chief Constable and the Deputy hurry to welcome him?' The writer then lamented the national divisions of the people. 'Disputes are raised, and the High Commissioner sits with a wide smile and wide open doors to receive the contenders, all too ready to win his favour and support by selling him the rights of their country ... The only winner in all this ... is the British High Commission. So long live England and her rights. Down with Egypt and all her rights!'

In 1928, the government could take no more of this and served a warning to the editor in these terms:

> Whereas the magazine *Rose al-Youssef*, with obnoxious material, wicked stories and indulgence in lies and fabrications, has established a disgraceful precedent harming the honour of the press and degrading ethics and morality, we have resolved:
> – To issue a warning to *Rose al-Youssef*.
> – To call on the magazine, *Rose al-Youssef*, to publish this warning in the next issue.
> – To instruct the Mayor of Cairo to implement this decision.

The magazine published the warning with this comment:

> We accept that we have established a disgraceful precedent ... But do we not have the right to ask our beloved ministry, or haven't the people the right to beg of their dear minister to instruct the Publications Department to issue a list of the lies ... which we must then avoid and spare the much aggrieved honour of the press from the disgraceful precedent which we so unfairly established. Did we, for example, tell a lie when we said that the monster of failure is creeping into this cabinet in silk slippers? Please advise us and Allah shall reward the good doers. If you don't, we shall, by God, have nothing other than God's patience to

cling to, the sea to drink from until satisfaction, and our hands to raise to heaven and pray that He may turn all liars into monkeys.

The government did not publish a list of the lies which should be avoided. Instead it promulgated, in 1933, a new law for the press which denied the treatment of journalists as political prisoners in any offence affecting any member of the royal family. *Rose al-Youssef* reported that a minister wanted to include also any of His Majesty's ministers. 'God shed his light on one of the members of this happy-go-lucky parliament to say that the parliament would raise no objection if its members were also included in the clause ... Tomorrow the British will ask that the provision should also apply to anyone swearing at a foreign power or sticking out his tongue at the High Commissioner's residency.'

The magazine was prosecuted and suspended many times, but nothing deflected it from its course of exposing the government and attacking the British domination. Its strong-headed independence finally led to a split from the Wafd Party which it had supported for so long. It did not like the Anglo–Egyptian Treaty negotiated by the Wafd in 1936, '... a treaty which secured for the British everything and gave the Egyptians nothing other than the right to fly their air force over London' (the reciprocal notion of the treaty). All that Britain did, it said, was to shift her luggage from one side of the ship to the other.

A series of cartoons followed in denunciation of the agreement and the Wafd Party. In one caricature, John Bull is shown sitting at the table with al-Misri Effendi (Mr Egyptian) and the Wafdist leader, Nahhas Pasha, who is asking the terrified Misri Effendi to pick up a snake (the treaty) on the table. 'It's true its bite is painful and fatal, but this is the smallest snake I could find you.' In another cartoon, Nahhas Pasha tells his colleague, Makram Ubaid Pasha: 'We lost the King's sympathy, lost the elections, lost our money, lost in the agreement, lost the friendship of the British, what is left for us to lose?' Makram Ubaid replies, 'We may still lose each other.'

Of course, high politics was not the only concern of *Rose al-Youssef*, which addressed itself also to all the incongruities of the transitional Arab society. Noting a small advertisement in one of Cairo's dailies offering fifteen pounds to anyone helping in the recovery of a lost ailing bitch called Lolo, the magazine used the opportunity to attack the frivolous bourgeoisie of Egypt:

A lady is offering fifteen pounds to anyone helping in the

recovery of a bitch . . . an ailing bitch. How much would she pay
had the bitch been in good health, with rosy cheeks, shining eyes,
swaying buttocks, buxom bosom, slim waist and a short tail . . .
But, oh good people, why did this pampered and beloved bitch get
lost? Her owner says that she was ailing . . . perhaps she was
afflicted with an illness which defeated the brilliance of our
physicians, drove Lolo to despair and prompted her to throw
herself in the River Nile . . .

   If my guess is true, perhaps Lolo's owner may send the fifteen
pounds to the Nur wa Rahma Orphanage in memory of the
mourned youth and soul of Lolo. Thus, she may bring pleasure to
the hearts of scores of small, deprived children. Fifteen pounds as
a reward for a dog while hundreds and thousands of children and
disabled folk are dying of hunger in this country. Oh, God
Almighty, strike this land with your wrath and vengeance.[7]

That was in 1927 when the writer of such columns had never dreamt
of earning fifteen pounds in a whole month.

   The success of *Rose al-Youssef* inspired many writers to branch
off into their own publications. In 1926, Dar al-Hilal launched
al-Fukaha (Humour) under the editorship of Hussein Shafiq who
epitomized the Egyptian brand of humour in this magazine, which
was later on changed into the famous *al-Ithnayn*, as an organ for the
serious and the frivolous. Among Hussein Shafiq's inventions was
'Our Court Martial', a satirical feature which exposed public figures
by submitting them to mock trials, a device which was copied by
other humorous journalists in the Arab World.

   This was a completely new departure in Arab public life and the
writers and readers alike were sailing into an uncharted sea, with
plenty of mud-slinging, until the ship hit the rocks in 1933, when
the Public Prosecutor decided to intervene and charged Muhammad
al-Tabi'i, editor of *Rose al-Youssef*, with indecency and had him put
in prison for four months. The court ruled that the humorous press
'was publishing immoral and indecent material with the claim that
it was frank literature. Diverse methods were used to propagate lies,
indulge in vilification, defamation and outright slander.' The
reference in this pronouncement was to the numerous stories of the
kind carried nowadays in Britain, for example, by *Private Eye* about
personal matters and private affairs.

   Al-Ahram joined in the condemnation and wrote, on 23 October
1933: 'The reports which *al-Sarih* is anxious to publish are trivialities,
but they are dangerous to decency and injurious to morality. We live

in an oriental country in which a man disdains the mention of the name of his wife, his sister or his daughter.' *Al-Ahram* was not althogether correct in this because, as already mentioned, attacking men by slandering their women folk has been always a common practice in the Middle East. Years later, in 1962, Anwar al-Jundi endorsed the condemnation and gave this explanation: 'No doubt', he said, 'that imperialism had a great share in expanding and strengthening this kind of journalism and in diverting the press from its innocent criticism and useful message to this form of disgraceful practice.' Innocence seems indeed to be the quality fervently adhered to by al-Jundi. He also found occasion to feel particularly incensed by the symbol of Egypt used by cartoon-ists in the form of an improperly dressed woman 'sometimes half naked and standing in a seductive pose in front of John Bull, the symbol of Britain. This is degrading and shameful!'[8]

The matter became a *cause célèbre*, as Egypt's intellectual and political figures joined in the affray. Muhammad Hussein Haikal, the Liberal leader,[9] attacked, in an article carried by the daily *al-Siyasa* on 30 May 1933, the style and subject matter of *Rose al-Youssef*. 'To encourage this kind of journalism is a crime against morality. Perhaps the worst damage done to the case of this country in the last ten years was the denigration of morality and the use of weapons, whatever they may be and however destructive they may prove to public morality, against the Egyptian political opponents.'

Taha Hussein replied on 31 May in *Kawkab al-Sharq* to this standpoint: 'Those who love democratic life and faithfully stand in guard of it must not enjoy its advantages and feel incensed by its disadvantages to this limit.' After drawing attention to the fact that when the same newspapers supported the Liberals and used exactly the same foul methods in beating their opponents, the Liberals raised no objection nor tried to prosecute them, Taha Hussein argued:

> It is not right that the political struggle is only the pure and innocent postulation of right, based purely and exclusively on the principles of morality and ethics. It is this, but there are also other things included like exposure to injury and the suffering of terrible injustice and outright violation. It is strange indeed that our friend Haykal imagines that I shall lose my patience if some of the newspapers say about me some of what has been said about the others these days. I do not know, my dear friend, of any one contemporary who has been mauled and vilified by both the

humorous and earnest press like myself. You remember, if you haven't already forgotten, that the serious and humorous press spent months and years talking of nothing except my person. They said about me whatever came into their minds without any accountability, control over their pens or sense of shame. Perhaps you remember, if you haven't already forgotten, that I turned my back on what they had said and I still do. I have not written against them, denounced them, brought them to justice or complained of them to the authorities. There is another way of dealing with the excessively humorous newspapers, and that is by answering their humour with humour and their trifling with trifling.

The eminent doctor went on to state that, in fact, the relationship between the Constitutional Liberals and the press was scandalous. This was too much for Haykal and he went on immediately to call on his opponent to specify and name these scandals. Taha Hussein gave his polite answer thus:

> I don't want to leaf through the pages of *al-Siyasa* itself. I am told it is a serious newspaper and I don't want to extract chapter and verse or some news reports from it. I don't want to expose the Publications Department, the articles which were written there and then fed to some of our newspapers. I don't want to mention the visits made, nor the banquets and late night revelries. I don't want to mention any of these things . . . I would rather be the vanquished in this situation a thousand times over than be the victor.[10]

This is all Mark Antony *à la* Taha Hussein! It is interesting to note the liberal use of 'my friend' among the sworn enemies in Arab polemics. In later years, the linguists and giants of modern Arab thought had another confrontation in which Muhammad Hussein Haykal decided to shift the battle to the more familiar ground of the same old grammatical fencing in which he tried to expose the professorship of Taha Hussein, by listing the idiomatic errors into which the doctor fell in his writings. Taha Hussein countered by listing the idiomatic mistakes of Haykal in his own article. Not a very encouraging thought for those who are trying to learn Arabic! Taha Hussein's career was surrounded with controversies and polemics which engulfed most of the leaders of Arab contemporary thought. His famous duel with Zaki Mubarak, as usual for personal reasons, prompted, in 1935, these lines from Dr Mubarak in the daily *al-Balagh*:

> For two years, Taha Hussein remained a shadow among the shadows of the political world. He has not left a single political party which he has not served and praised in long colourful letters. Political attitudes are parts of the mental attitude and the man who wavers from one political creed to another cannot be far off from becoming a victim of bewilderment *vis-à-vis* the literary schools. The very good man Taha Hussein served three political parties before the war and four after . . . He is an imitator in everything. Just look at the way he shrugs his shoulders like the French.

Zaki Mubarak did not explain how the totally blind Taha Hussein managed to imitate the French way of shoulder shrugging, but went on reaffirming his oath, 'If I ever find my children hungry, I shall roast Taha Hussein for them.'[11] Perhaps the biggest joke in Taha Hussein's career was the way in which he was forced to recant and confirm: 'I believe in God, his books, his prophets, his angels, his Day of Judgement and that all good and bad are from the Most High.'

Muhammad al-Tabi'i, whose articles kindled the earlier controversy, seems to have enjoyed the fray and thrived on imprisonment, for in 1934 he branched off to start his own satirical newspaper, *Akhir Sa'a* (The Last Hour) in which writers like Mustafa Amin and Ahmad al-Sawi acquired their initial fame. By then many journalists began to jump on the bandwagon as they discovered the popularity and success of the humorous press and the fat salaries earned by the caricaturists and witty columnists. Whereas the editor-in-chief of the prestigious *al-Ahram* earned thirty pounds a month, *Rose al-Youssef*'s editor was paid five hundred pounds.

A typical example of al-Tabi'i's satirical rhetoric is his attack on the old phenomenon of the time-servers and political hypocrites, as he wrote on 26 April 1942.

> In Egypt, there are honourable colleagues who have been able to work in journalism and politics for years and years without losing one single friend or making one single enemy among our leaders and the chieftains of our political parties. This is a pleasing gift and skill for which some of them may receive congratulations, albeit from men with no ethical standards. The method followed by such honourable colleagues is to praise

every prime minister and every leader with the same sentiments
and terms . . .

If Sa'ad Zaghlul, Mustafa al-Nahhas, Hilmi Isa, Ali Mahir,
Muhammad Mahmud, Ismael Sidqi, Hussein Sirri and Ahmad
Mahir are all prophets of patriotism, fountains of generosity, men
of efficiency, great Egyptian patriots, true in their determination
and aspirations to serve their country and uphold her constitution, who have then violated, suspended and annulled the
constitution of Egypt, falsified her will and subjected her to
humiliation, dishonour and a parliament so lofty in name and so
ignoble in spirit?

If these leaders are equal in the opinion of these honourable
colleagues, and deserve equal praise and descriptions as sublime
examples to be recorded on the same page of the glorious annals
of history, and as high ideals of righteous rule, disinterested spirit
and devotion to Egypt and her constitution, who is responsible
then for this squalid mess accumulated between 1924 and 1942?
Who is responsible for these demolished pillars in the monument
in Egypt's rise? Who hath done that, O Abraham, to our gods?'

Akhir Sa'a was not a radical magazine nor did it seek confront-
ations with the establishment or champion the cause of the
deprived, as *Rose al-Youssef* did. In fact, it operated basically within
the context of the establishment and allocated extensive columns
to the news and gossip of high society, but some of its gem society
reports had their real sharp edges as in the following specimens:

– The telephone rang at Mahmud Shakir Pasha's home. When His
Excellency answered the phone, the caller, the secretary of the
Minister of Justice, informed him that the minister had arranged for
him a meeting at 10 a.m. Shakir Pasha answered: 'You must have the
wrong number. I haven't asked for such a meeting.' That His
Excellency assumed the telephone number to be wrong is not
surprising. He was the Director General of Telegraph and
Telephones.

– Aziz Sidqi is awaiting the birth of a son in the next few weeks,
endowed with all the instant signs of genius. It is reported that His
Excellency Sidqi Pasha has already reserved a high position for the
baby in the Suez Canal Company.

– In the last fortnight the daughter of His Excellency Fu'ad Bey
Shirin married Maître Muhammad Hathiq. It is said that the
bridegroom brought such good omens that no sooner was he married
to her than a Royal Decree was issued appointing her father a

Governor of al-Qallubia. The rest is on the way, as the saying goes.

– His Excellency Hussein Sirri Pasha, the Minister of Finance, forgot his glasses when he left the ministry. The following day he found them restored to his desk without any harm, but His Excellency rang the bell and called for his private secretary.

– What's your name?

– Such and such.

– What age are you?

– Such and such.

– What is your job?

– Your Excellency's Secretary.

– No, you are no use as a secretary and no use at anything.

– Why, Your Excellency?

– How did you discover that I had forgotten my glasses and yet forget to clean them? Get out! You are fired.

The paradoxical problems of dragging up a developing nation from its medieval modes were also expansively noted. As the government prohibited the ugly scenes of the bereaved women following the funeral processions of their dear lost ones with their hysterics and histrionics, the magazine reported the uglier scenes of the confrontation between the police and the female mourners:

The result of this decision was a series of embroilments following every coffin with the screams of the women rising higher and higher. The position of the police officer became untenable as he stood between two fires: to carry out his orders and turn the single funeral into a double and the deceased into two dead men, the lamented deceased who had already died and the officer who is struck dead with embarrassment, or to ignore the orders of his government . . .

Last week, such a funeral was proceeding followed by women with blackened faces screaming 'Oh, me lion, me leopard . . . to witness your day! Me dear, me darlin' . . . ' A police officer barred their passage and one of them exclaimed, 'Oh, why Omar?' The officer replied that it was the order of the Ministry of Social Affairs, upon which the woman in question raised her lament even higher, 'Oh, why, O Omar! The Angel of Death's now transferred to the Shosal Effails you speak of?!'

The officer could only smile and withhold his tongue as the woman went on: 'Oh, me lion, me husband, leavin' us with yer death to any worthy an' unworthy. Leavin' us to the Monstery of Shosal Effails to gloat over us. Oh, our ruin!'

Despite *Akhir Sa'a's* benign criticism, the famous Cairo weekly was suspended, in 1939, for three months and its editor went on to address himself to its readers on 4 February 1940:

This is a happy occasion in which we meet you again with the return of *Akhir Sa'a* to the field of struggle after three month's absence which it has spent loitering in the winter resorts of our happy Nile. First, we are well and extremely anxious to speak to you. May you and your children be in best condition. Secondly, we were looking for someone to whom we can address this message and speak of our woes of the last three months, but we could find none other than you.

We tried to send it to our critics, but they said anything but. He who throws himself in the fire must bear its burning, and he who exposes himself to cold should not complain of influenza. Therefore, we said, let us send it to the Prime Minister. We had hardly uttered the first verse when we felt, for some reason or another, that we were embraced with blank looks ... We tried to write to the Minister of the Exterior, or the Minister of the Interior, but they said to us, 'Good day! Have you forgotten that God has gathered the whole world in one? The Prime Minister works with three souls in one.'

We considered writing to the Minister of Social Affairs. He is a good man. But we discovered that the best words to describe His Excellency now is that he has become like a haystack – voluminous but trifling. Then we thought of addressing our complaint to the Minister of *Awqaf* (religious endowments) but we found that the New Order introduced by His Excellency al-Hajjaj bin Yusif al-Shathili did not allow even the letters of the public to climb the stairs without colliding with an army of bureaucrats and doormen whose only function in the ministry seems to be to ask any caller on his entry and departure: Wherefrom are you? Whereto do you intend? Wherefore is your visit? Who are you? Who is your God? What is your faith? What religion have you died in? Just like the angels on the Day of Reckoning!

We tried to write to the Minister of Defence, the Minister of Education, the Minister of Justice, to any minister whatsoever, but we found all doors shut before us and the sword drawn up in every corner ... They have all become like the doves of the Qa'ba Mosque: no one is allowed to touch them.

At last, we could not but think of you, dear reader ... There are things brewing in our minds and you have your intelligence. Try to read between the lines some of what we wish to tell you. If you can't, then compensate for what you have missed with an hour in which you may read *The Book of Aspirations* by al-Qali, *The Book of Animals* by al-Jahiz or *The Literature of the World and Religion*. They are all worthy books printed on good-quality paper, illustrated with pictures and sold for a total price of less than one year's subscription to our esteemed magazine.

The editorial was accompanied by a questionnaire which resulted in support for the magazine by ninety-seven per cent of the readers. It seems that Nasser's and Sadat's claims of ninety-nine per cent mass support were really only a continuation of well established traditions.

With the outbreak of World War II and the Axis invasion of Egypt, the censor clamped down on publication and the development of the satirical press suffered another setback, but, with the characteristic sense of humour of Egypt, the humorists found new sources of harmless inspiration. *Akhir Sa'a* noted that the official pricing of essential needs had not included hashish, but the omission had not resulted in any tangible appreciation in its black-market price. This seems to have allowed the proverbial *hashshashin* (hashish addicts) of Cairo to augment their arsenal of bottomless humour with a new source of jokes about the war. Hearing that the Germans had halted their advance to service and clean their tanks, one *hashshash* asked another, 'Why don't the allies attack them now while they are busy cleaning their tanks?'

'Because the allies don't like dirt,' said the other.

A third one related that a German officer heard the air-raid siren and hurried to hide under his bed, but he found his wife's lover there. 'What are you doing here?'

'I am only hiding from the air raid,' said the lover.

'Get out of here. This is my place.' The lover rushed out and rejoined the wife on top . . .

The caricaturists joined the public in treating the blackout and the whole war as a series of jokes. In one cartoon, a man is seen smashing his bicycle in anger. 'Why are you doing that?' asked his mate.

'I am sick of it,' said the owner. 'Last week I was fined for cycling without lights. This week I am fined for cycling with lights!'

Reporting the lights coming from a mosque, a policeman in another cartoon knocked at the door and enquired: 'Whose house is this?'

'God's!' answered the Imam.

The war witnessed the rising star of *al-Ba'kuka*, a weekly newspaper completely devoted to humour and including many native features like *al-Qafiya* (Egyptian rhyme quiz), but its pro-establishment line ran against the new militant spirit of opposition and anti-royalist agitation, which blunted its satirical edge and left it behind the trends of post-war Egypt. Its place was filled by *Kilma was Nus* and *sabah al-Khayr*. Of course, there were other weekly magazines like *al-Ithnayn* and *al-Misri Effendi*, published by Abd al-Rihman Nasr and edited by Ma'mun al-Shinnawi, which followed *Akhir Sa'a*'s track by mixing the serious with the funny.

For many years the Egyptian press was the primary source of enlightened and mature reading in the Arab World, and the development of the satirical and humorous publications was bound to make its impact on the other countries. Indeed, when Nuri Thabit applied for a licence to issue his own humour newspaper in Iraq, he referred to *al-Kashkul* and *Rose al-Youssef* and said that it was high time for Iraq to have similar publications. But Nuri Thabit was not the first pioneer of the satirical press in Iraq. As a matter of fact, Michael Tays published in the same year in which *Rose al-Youssef* appeared, the first satirical weekly in Baghdad with the title of *Kannas al-Shawari'* (The Road Sweeper). 'My plan,' Tays wrote in introducing his newspaper, 'is as clear as the sun in the midst of night. I shall carry my broom and roam the streets and winding lanes. Wherever I see someone committing something injurious to taste, smell, public order, law and the fiddle, I shall strike him on the head. If my broom is broken it will be my loss. If his head is broken, it will be his.'

It would be interesting to note that Michael Tays was another of those pioneers falling under the impact of Western education. He was a Christian graduate from the American Jesuit College in Baghdad. But Tays was unfortunate enough to try that kind of writing in Iraq, and only a few months later he almost died from an assassin's bullet as a result.[12]

With that bullet ended the first experiment as Tays retreated from this bloody field of journalism. His steps, however, were followed by Khalaf Shawqi al-Dawoodi who issued *Qarandal*. Among the series of articles which achieved great popularity were 'Al-Iraq Shlaun Yisawik Taraqqi', or 'Iraq, how can we civilize you?' but said with the broken Arabic of a Bengali officer of the British Indian Army. The jokes were mainly verbal, but were immensely appreciated by the Iraqis as they followed the same beaten track of xenophobia and chauvinism. The Iraqis had been used to seeing Indian Muslims coming to the holy places as beggars at their mercy. To see them now as officers ordering about the natives with the authority of the British mandate and the assumption of civilizing the country was for them a situation full of ironies and funny inversions. Khalaf Shawqi, I hardly need add, was not shot by his compatriots.

The newspaper which had a more lasting reputation was *Habazbuz*, issued by Nuri Thabit in 1931 with the professed intention of attacking the social ills without seeking political confrontation with the authorities. 'God forbid!' Its kind of humour may be summed up in the following extract. A man was seen passing water and was stopped by the night watchman.

– Effendi, what are you doing?
– Only pissing on this mud. What is it to do with you!
– How can you piss on mud? Isn't it blessed by God?
– How peculiar. How can you say mud is blessed by God?
– May we thank the Almighty for leaving us alive! Wasn't it from mud that God made Adam?

The argument is not about public health or decency, but about desecrating the holy mud. In a descriptive piece, he attacked the same target of the westernized man-about-town:

He stands bare headed, winter and summer, with greasy combed hair shining in the sun like a piece of patent leather. For his long sideboards, he has to borrow some five centimetres from his beard. His cheeks are flushed with powder and rouge and perhaps with a touch of lipstick or walnut peel on his mouth, like any cheap woman. His long collar is dangling like the ears of an ass over a tie as wide as a bathroom towel. All this because the gentleman is an amateur actor. Thus he wears a jacket too narrow and too short to cover his bottom which he dresses up in a Charleston pantaloon with such width and size as may accommodate two or more of Abu Hamad's thighs in each side.

Habazbuz's anecdotes and comments were remembered and cited by Iraqis for many years after the death of its founder and end of its publication in 1940. The one joke I remember from Nuri Thabit was the one he related when his son asked him, 'Dad, all these prostitutes in the Kallachia, sleeping with men all night through, don't they get pregnant? Don't they get children?' 'Of course they do', answered the father, 'Where do you think all these coachmen and taxi drivers come from then?'

Among the notable contributors to *Habazbuz* was Ibrahim Salih Shukr who distinguished himself with a critical assessment in a series of articles about some leading figures of the Arabi Revolt of Sharif Hussein, published under the title 'The Minister's Pen'. The pen here refers to the pen presented to the writer by the minister Ali Jawdat al-Ayubi. The development of the Iraqi satirical press was resumed after the war and a measure of democracy introduced with the publication of the weekly magazine *Al-Wadi* by Khalid al-Durra. The most notable feature in this weekly, which attracted widespread acclaim, was 'In the Dock', a series of mock trials exposing the faults and failings of various politicians. The magazine gave the opportunity to the artist Hamid al-Mahal to show his talent in the art of the caricature. Hamid al-Mahal was also an actor and a founder member of the Zabania Company which specialized in comedies, and this provided once more the same link which bound together the theatre, comedy, caricature and political humour. In fact, many of Iraq's latterday ministers and leaders, like Najib al-Rawi, Ahmad al-Rawi and Sadiq al-Bassam, spent their youth on the stage and helped to form the early theatrical company under the auspices of the National Party in 1921. Among the other co-founders was the same Nuri Thabit of *Habazbuz* who wrote a few social comedies including *Roben the Money-changer* (1926), considered by the historian of the Iraqi theatre, Dr Ali al-Zubaidi, to be the first legitimate comedy written in Iraq. The play attacked the same character of the usurer.[13]

Iraq is not a country famous for its sense of humour and it is more associated in the minds of other Arabs with violence and intolerance. Iraqi columnists had to battle against such traits without the backing of any assets in the fields of theatre or democracy, and fell into the expected mistake of thinking that slang is automatically funny and that writing in vernacular Arabic means writing something witty. They wrote with the added difficulty of using the vernacular dialect of Iraq which lacks the delicacy of the Egyptian dialect. The field in which the language of the Iraqis excels – swearing and obscenities – and which produced gems of Abbasid literature, was barred to them under the puritanical influences of nineteenth-century Europe. I have compared the obscenity and swear words of many peoples, both in the original and in translation, and could not but give the Iraqis first-rate credit in this race.

One day a prime minister was criticized by his colleagues for swearing rather too much and with the most vulgar of terms. The prime minister turned to the oldest in the company. 'I don't swear more than anyone else, do I Uncle?'

The old man answered: 'I really don't know much about you, but I remember well your father, may God rest him in peace. One day he was fasting during Ramadan and passing its long hours with reading the Qur'an. You were a little boy and started rowing with your mum and calling her all sorts of names. Recognizing that it was the sacred month and he was reading the holy book, he could bear it no longer. He closed the book and pointed it at her and said, 'Woman! Will you control this son of a whore or do you want me to stuff this Holy Qur'an up your cunt?' The reader should by no means wonder about the authenticity of the words used, for the Iraqis – and indeed Arabs in general – often use 'son of a whore' as an expression of great admiration for a politician, a leader, or a general. At other times, it is a term of great love and friendship for someone really dear to you. But the term is the prerogative of an Arab, and no foreigner, I should warn, may give himself the same liberty. As it happened, the prime minister in question shook his head in the negative. No, he could not remember the episode.

Perhaps, the sacrilegious nature of the Iraqis is best examplified in that famous chant: 'And He boasts that He created the camel!' which the tribesmen of that country sarcastically sang in the twenties about the Almighty as they were overwhelmed with the sight of the first aeroplane and improvised the blasphemous parody of the Qur'anic verse, 'And look you at the camels and how He created them.'

In Syria the longest published satirical publication was *Al-Mudhhik al-Mubki* (The Weeping Joker) which was published by Habib Kahhala for the first time in 1929 and continued for thirty-six years during which the magazine was suspended by the French authorities for a total of ten years. During the same period, Adib al-Taqi distinguished himself as one of Syria's wittiest poets, writing many an amusing poem like the one about the collapse of the new paper currency:

Do not feel downcast for your fall,
We live in an epoch of downfall.

In 1948, the League of Satirists was formed by twelve writers, but their enterprise was soon frozen with the new cold wind of change as the military took command of the country. A new approach to political satire, more guarded and cunning, was developed by a new

generation of writers among whom the most distinguished is
Zakaria Tamer. Basically a short-story writer, he used the art of
fiction and parable to point his accusing finger at the insolence of
office. Typical is his innuendo in one of his short stories about the
education of the present generation of Arab schoolchildren: 'There
are one million people. One hundred and fifty have been hanged,
how many are still in hand?'

In 1977, the authorities made a pact with him based on a
compromise which gave him a column in the daily newspaper
Tishrin (October). This new venture was given the title of 'The Tales
of Juha the Damascene', in which he resurrected the old Juha
anecdotes and recharged them with political contents.

Thus the king asks Juha for his opinion about his donkey.

'The king's donkey is the King of Donkeys,' replies Juha, and the
impressed king insists on Juha teaching the beast proper speech, a
task which is duly performed with the result that Juha learns how to
bray, while the ass accedes to the throne on the death of the king and
soon proves to be the best king that has ever ruled the country.

In another encounter between the two, the king asks Juha for his
advice on forming a new government, and the clown advises him
thus: there must be a Minister of Candles, whose job is to provide
the public with free candles to read the government gazette, another
Minister for Life and Death whose job is to publish reports that
health and recovery are in the hands of God, a third Minister for
Public Decency whose responsibility is to educate the people that it
is indecent to resist oppression and that anger against injustice
should be channelled into campaigning against pornography.

Gradually, the hints became more and more obvious and direct
until the authorities had to act and ban Zakaria Tamer, forcing him
in the end to follow the track of other intellectuals to the world of
Arab exile in London, where he resumed his style in a series of
articles published by *al-Tadhamun* under the old fitting title of 'The
Weeping Joker'.

In Tunisia, the satirical press was revolutionized in 1932 with the
return of the colloquial poet Bayram al-Tunisi, who published in
collaboration with other native humorists *al-Shabab* (The Youth).
Bayram used to write its editorials, compose the *malzumat* (a form of
Tunisian slang poetry) and give ideas to its caricaturist, Omar
al-Gharayiri. The newspaper followed the peculiar policy of refusing
to accept subscriptions, which Bayram justified by saying that it was
better for him to write 500 lines which put him in prison than to
spend his time in writing the names of the arrogant subscribers.

True enough, Bayram was arrested and exiled to France and the newspaper was banned, but during his brief stay in Tunis, he helped to form the *Taht al-sur* group of comic writers and satirists who went on to publish *al-Surur*.

The Tunisian satirical press had a long history extending to the beginning of this century, but most of the publications were soon stopped by the French authorities for one reason or another, with the exception of *al-Nadim*, which continued from 1921 to 1940. As elsewhere in the Arab World, *al-Nadim* and the majority of these publications used a combination of classical and slang Arabic to attack the intrusion of the Western way of life into Muslim society, and agitated for the independence of the country.

Here again we had the same ironical situation in which independence led to the banishment of its champions. The satirical press disappeared in Tunisia as it did in Egypt and other state-controlled societies where the press has been nationalized, and journalists and writers have become the paid hirelings of the government – as dull, ineffective and corrupt as its civil servants.

War Time Shortages
  'Every time you hear of a fire breaking out somewhere you dash there. Why?'
  'To light my cigarette.'
Al-Ithnayn 1944.

4 The Age of Resurgence: the Men of Wit

> Nothing is more significant of men's character than what
> they find as laughable.
>
> Goethe

The introduction of parliamentary life in the Arab World made the characteristic impact on the quality of politics and politicians and produced a new breed of witty statesmen. The Arabs had their satirical rulers like the Imam Ali and al-Hajjaj, men steeped in the traditions of oratory, poetry and autocracy, but they had no Richard Sheridan, Benjamin Franklin or Disraeli, men of repartee and gallant wit. Such types are a comparatively recent development in the world of political literature and are a direct result of free discussion held by gentlemen according to the rules of parliamentary democracy. Under the constitutional monarchies, the Arabs showed once more what their oral genius could produce in response to the exigencies and potentials of the day. Of such men, Sa'ad Zaghlul, the national leader and architect of Egyptian independence, comes to the fore. A liberal, a patriot, and an enlightened leader, he was typical of the new genre of politicians with their Western education and fervent nationalism.

Like many of the bright middle-class boys, Sa'ad studied law in Cairo before proceeding to Paris to finish his education and return kindled with the desire to arouse his people, secure independence and dignity for his country, advocate the cause for democracy, constitutional rule and parliamentary life and call for the co-existence of the cross and the crescent. He was one of the first Muslim politicians who allowed their wives to sit with colleagues and join in their discussions, and his telling gesture was more than adequately rewarded by Safiya, *Um al-Misriyin* (Mother of the Egyptians). Sa'ad had no children and this was rather hard on a woman in a land where women were normally honoured by calling them after their children, Um (mother of) so and so. Observing what looked to them like a sad omission, Sa'ad's supporters decided to make amends by calling her *Um al- Misriyin,* and indeed Safiya did act like the Mother of the Egyptians. Her house was continuously invaded by all sorts of people seeking advice, bringing in reports and joining in the endless discussions. At one meeting, a hot-headed young man lost his temper and used abusive words against another. Sa'ad Zaghlul had to step in and ask the youngster to behave himself: 'How dare you say such things in my own house?'

'This is not your house', replied the young man, 'this is the house of the nation.'

And *Bayt al-Umma* has remained the name given by the Egyptians to Sa'ad's house ever since. Although he was no advocate of public nationalization, he had thus his entire household, wife and hearth publicly nationalized.

Safiya made good practical use of her 'motherhood' on at least one occasion. When the British police arrested many activists, they allowed only close relatives to see the detainees, among whom many had no relatives available to see them – a rather hard situation as they could have decent food only when it was brought to them by their visitors. Safiya packed a few baskets and went to see them and the prison warden asked her to identify her relationship with any of the prisoners. 'I am their mother,' Safiya replied. The Mother of the Egyptians had obviously an ample share of her husband's eloquence as when she expressed her dislike of the monarchy. On a royal occasion to unveil the statue of Sa'ad Zaghlul after his death, Safiya was designated to sit, not on the right of the monarch as customary, but with the other women in their secluded pavilion. She rejected the arrangement not out of personal vanity, but in deference to the whole movement of women's emancipation for which she and her husband had worked. 'Tell His Majesty,' she said, 'it will do him great honour to sit by me. It won't do me any honour to sit by him.[1] The impasse was resolved by the king being honoured and the women of Egypt standing their ground.

Sa'ad Zaghlul was a disciple of the enigmatic Jamal al-Din al-Afghani, the religious reformer who made a great impression on the intellectuals of his time, and Sa'ad was described as the best exponent of his mentor's ideas on freedom and enlightenment. Therefore, when the Arabi Revolt took place he had no hesitation in supporting it. During his more mature years, he expressed great admiration for Mukhtar's monument 'Egypt Resurgent' representing a female peasant awakening the sphinx, and said that it should be placed at the most important square in Cairo. He was advised against collecting donations for the project as it could incense the clergy who might treat it as idolatry and blasphemy. 'Why,' he replied, 'the clergy did not object to seeing the statue of the Khedive Muhammad Ali erected in Alexandria and the statue of the Khedive Ibrahim Pasha erected in Cairo!'

As it happened, 'Egypt Resurgent' was confiscated by the British after the 1919 uprising and was put in store. The statue remained under lock and key for eight years and Sa'ad could not fail to observe, 'The statue is now the only political prisoner still under arrest.'

The confrontation with the British was bound to lead to his exile and the expected knock at the door was finally heard. 'You are rather late,' he said to the officer with the warrant for his arrest. 'I've been expecting you for a long time.'

The officer replied, 'My orders are to arrest Your Excellency at 5 p.m. and it is now 5 p.m.'

The Arab joke was lost on the Englishman who marched off with his charge, looking rather awkward and embarrassed. Observing them from his café, a local wit remarked, 'To me, they seem to march with the British officer under the arrest of Sa'ad Zaghlul.'[2] Looking at the warrant issued by General Allenby and bearing his signature under 'Your most obedient servant', Sa'ad grinned. 'Typical of the hypocrisy of an Englishman! He grabs me by the scruff of the neck to the point of strangulation and then tells me that he is my most obedient servant!'

He was finally exiled with other national leaders to Malta and the impact of the painful separation on their wives kept worrying the exiles until Sa'ad was inspired with this suggestion. Let everyone write to his wife and tell her that he has taken a Maltese woman for a seond wife! She would soon forget him.

But Safiya neither forgot nor gave up as she proved to be a master propagandist in orchestrating a national campaign with the simple crisp reply to the British measure, *Yahya Sa'ad* (Long live Sa'ad) shouted everywhere, chalked on every wall, rubber-stamped on every paper and banknote; the whole country was chanting the one chorus of *Yahya Sa'ad*. The Egyptians mixed their sense of humour with their sense of superstition. Rumour had it that the bean shoots were appearing with *Yahya Sa'ad* inscribed on their leaves miraculously by Allah. Then there was the medical report that while examining a pregnant woman, a doctor heard through his stethoscope the foetus whimpering *Yahya Sa'ad*. The amazed doctor, obviously lacking in his religious faith, invited another colleague who confirmed the phenomenon.[3]

Britain tried to clinch a deal with some local lackey and, indeed, opened negotiations with the government of Adli Yakun. Upon hearing of this attempt, Sa'ad coined the phrase which entered the Arab political jargon, 'George V negotiates with George V'. Whitehall had no option but to release him and eventually invite him to London for talks. Facing an English audience and trying to be diplomatic and conciliatory, he was at a loss to find something to say which united the British and the Egyptians. He finally went back more than two thousand years to find something in common. 'If we invoked the soul of Julius Caesar, we should find no two countries in whose rule he had so much trouble as Egypt and England.'

His biographer and assistant, Abbas Mahmud al-Aqqad, descibed him as courageous, frank and skilful, and compared him with Lloyd George in his wit and sense of humour. The two statesmen met and the British Prime Minister asked him what his intentions were *vis-à-vis* the foreigners and the British. 'Friendship towards all foreigners, even the British.' Intending to smooth the talks, Lloyd George volunteered a kind interpretation of 'even the British'. 'I think you mean friendship with all of them but especially the British.'[4] The Arabs had maintained a suspicious attitude towards Lloyd George and considered him as the source of their recurring crisis. A British journalist reported to Sa'ad what the British Prime Minister had said about him: 'The health of Sa'ad Pasha thrives on crisis.' Sa'ad replied: 'May God give him a long life.' Lloyd George's observation seems to have been more kind than correct, for the health of the great Egyptian was actually in decline and his talks with England were cut short by his death in 1927.

Not everybody would agree with al-Aqqad's comparison, but one quality common to Arabs and Celts may indeed be shared by the two Welsh and Arab orators, i.e. their predilection for the picturesque. 'There are people among the people who, upon seeing a man beating and the beaten crying, say to the man being beaten, "Do not cry!" before saying to the man who is beating him, "Do not beat him",' is one of the pieces learnt by Arab children as a sample of Sa'ad's oratory and eloquence. In describing a tiresome supporter, he said, 'He is like the mucus in your nose. You feel disgusted when you get it out, and you feel disgusted when you leave it in.'

The foregoing words sum up Sa'ad Zaghlul's tolerance, and he was quite right when he said that he was prepared to endure even his opponents, an attitude which manifested itself in his dealings with the press. He was the first Arab prime minister to give a press interview, notwithstanding his poor opinion of pressmen.

Commenting on al-Manfaluti's description of journalists as writers who express their opinions in dribs and drabs without a total comprehensive meaning, he added that they were 'retailers and not wholesalers'. The words may have a commercial undertone in view of the frequent practice of Arab journalists, of which he was quite aware. He dealt with them on another occasion when he said that freedom had made great advances in Egypt. Guests used to eat from what the prince ate and leave what the prince left. Now they are eating everything! Enquiring after a journalist who fell ill, he was told that the man suffered a stomach condition. 'Perhaps he has swallowed one of his articles.'

His sincere devotion to democracy had never clouded his perception of its ironies in a developing country. A man came to wish his Wafd Party success in the election. 'Why not? If we win, he will come for his reward. If we lose he will never show us his face again,' said Sa'ad, and went on to relate the story of his mentor al-Afghani when his ship was caught in a violent storm. Al-Afghani calmed his fellow travellers by prophesying to them, on the strength of his proximity to God, that nothing would happen to the ship. 'If the ship sinks,' al-Afghani told his companion, 'no one will live to tell the tale of my lie. If she survives, I shall win belief in my holiness.' That is how, Sa'ad drew the lesson, the people believed in the green turban of the shaykh.

In another instance, Sa'ad went on praising Uthman Muharram, his Minister of Public Works, and recommending him to a junior engineer at the ministry. When they were both gone, Lutfi al-Sayid gasped, 'I'd understand if you recommended the junior engineer to the minister, not the minister to the engineer!' Sa'ad's reply was, 'Uthman Muharram is an MP for Dassuq. This young engineer is an elector in that constituency.'

Sa'ad was very gentle, compassionate and understanding. He once had a deputy who was in the habit, typical of all Arabs, of shouting when making a long-distance call. As the deputy was often speaking to Alexandria his telephone calls became quite irksome to Sa'ad. He called for his secretary: 'Tell His Excellency that he has no need to shout to Alexandria. There is now a telephone which he can use!' A woman came to see him about her husband and went on listing all the foul deeds which he had done her. 'Really these matters are no concern of mine,' he told her. The woman then turned the direction of her complaints to listing all the foul things which her husband had said about him. 'And these matters are no concern of yours,' he told her.

As Minister of Education, Sa'ad Zaghlul played an important role in shaping the future course of education in Egypt and turning that country into a trendsetter and cultural centre for the Arab World. He did this with vigorous despatch of graduates to Europe, so much so that the religious seminar of Al-Azhar complained of excluding its clerical scholars from the missions. 'Where can I send them to study Islam? To the Vatican?' The extent of Sa'ad's mature understanding of learning may be contrasted with the present-day practice of Arab students actually coming to Europe and America to study their own religion.

Observing that an applicant for a scholarship to study abroad was married and advanced in age, he asked him how he was going to manage as a man with a family. 'I shall divorce her, Your Excellency,' replied the man. Sa'ad scribbled on his application, 'Not to be trusted with the education of our children.' Once more it is interesting to contrast this attitude with the more recent measures of some Arab governments to encourage men to divorce their wives for various political reasons.

Sa'ad Zaghlul was in turn compared with Faris al-Khuri, the great Syrian statesman, but the comparison ends at their frequent use of humour in pursuit of the political cause of their countries. Otherwise, they are different both in style and outlook. Sa'ad was inherently an Egyptian whereas al-Khuri was more pan-Arab and his wit was more in keeping with traditional Arab humour. But like Sa'ad, Bourguiba and many other witty politicians of the contemporary Arab World, he was a lawyer and derived a great deal of his style from the tools of his profession. Typical of his characteristically Arabic style is his frequent resort to verbiage, and especially puns. Alas, most of his jokes and jibes in this genre are untranslatable. However, he was once summoned by the French High Commissioner for teaching revolution to his students when he was a professor at the Faculty of Law. Al-Khuri availed himself of the perennial problems of French-Arabic translation and pronunciation and said, 'No, I was wrongly reported. I was not teaching them revolution but evolution.' It may be amusing for us to note that a descendant of the French Revolution should ban the discussion of revolution at a law college.

Faris Al-Khuri was described as an exceptionally intelligent statesman and the Syrians pointed to the size of his head as a proof of their claim. It was said that he always had difficulty in finding a fez large enough to fit him. Thus he once spent a whole day shopping around in search of a suitable fez until he eventually found one which fitted him. The shopkeeper, however, asked a price which al-Khuri recognized as exhorbitant – and said so to the shopkeeper. 'Sir, if you find another fez in the whole of Damascus which will fit your head, you can have this one free,' said the shopkeeper. 'My dear friend,' said al-Khuri, 'if you find another head in the whole of Syria which fits your fez, charge the man whatever you like.'

Another characteristically Arab feature of his humour is his resort to parables in driving home a point or debunking an argument. The full flower of his brilliance was exhibited at the United Nations when he represented his country soon after independence, and many delegates still cherish memories of the exhilarating moments of his speeches. Syria was still occupied by both France and Britain and the Syrians were demanding the withdrawal of their forces. Lord Cadogan, the delegate of the United Kingdom, defended the presence of British troops in Syria by saying that they were there to prevent any clashes between the French troops and the Syrians. Al-Khuri gave his reply by recalling that this was really the story of the man with the lamp. Why do you hang this lamp on this post every night, the man was asked.

'In order to warn people against stumbling against the post.'

'And why do you have this post there,' they asked him.

'I need it to hang the lamp!'

Many foreigners feel irked by the Arabs with their repeated invocation of the Palestine case and the rights of the Palestinians, but they usually understand the Arab grievance and put up with the tedious representation of the case. Mr Andrei Vyshinsky, the Soviet delegate at the United Nations was not, however, prepared to show that kind understanding, and attacked the Syrian delegate for his repeated reference to Palestine and for reopening the case every day. Faris al-Khuri answered Vyshinsky by telling him the story of the married couple who went to court. The husband complained to the judge that he was a poor man and yet his wife kicked up a fuss every morning demanding a guinea from him. The judge asked her whether this was true. 'Yes, it is true Your Honour. I kick up a fuss every morning demanding a guinea; but I am not asking him to give me a guinea every morning. I am only asking him to give me one guinea once in our lifetime.'[5]

The Arabs must feel really dejected and frustrated when they recall, as I have recalled, these giants of Arab thought and national resurgence and compare them with the nonentities who speak for them now and run their affairs. So much was indeed felt and expressed most eloquently by another contemporary Arab wit, the

famous Egyptian journalist, Mustafa Amin, whose name is associated
with all the satirical and humorous magazines and newspapers of
his country and whose ideas, according to the cartoonist Rakha,
were behind most of the caricature characters like Ibn al-Balad, the
simple citizen who defies all rules in defence of justice and common
sense. After studying political science in the United States, Mr
Amin returned to Cairo to join *Rose al-Youssef*, *Akhir Sa'a* and
al-Ithnayn and came to the conclusion eventually that his real place
was in journalism, not in political science. He therefore launched
the successful *Akhbar al-Yaum*. To me, he represents one of the
happiest marriages of Western culture and oriental tradition,
reflected in his sincere adherence to the values of Western
democracy, liberty and free enterprise, on the one hand, and a sober
belief in God and Islam on the other. He said that he found himself
always in the habit of repeating in his sleep *Ya rabb* (O God). Yet his
religiosity did not prevent him from seeing the funny side of
religious mania. He related many amusing details about the lives
and beliefs of the four Muslim Brothers he met in gaol. Each of them
wanted to lead the prayers and hastened to announce the *athan* that
little bit before the rest. The result was that the five daily prayers
went on creeping forward a few minutes every day. 'If this
competition continues,' Mustafa Amin observed, 'the midday prayer
will be made at dawn and the evening prayer at noon.' His humour is
also a wonderful marriage of the Anglo-Saxon and the Egyptian.
What better luck can any humorist hope for? Typical of his remarks
was the answer which he gave to a reporter asking various public
figures about their best means of overcoming insomnia. 'I rarely
suffer from insomnia ... But when I do, I pick up one of my articles in
al-Ithnayn. That soon sends me to sleep.'

His pro-Western or, more precisely, pro-American politics were
bound to clash with the new trends of the Arab nationalist
movement with its emphasis on nationalization, socialism and anti-
Americanism. With the increased tension between Cairo and
Washington, Mustafa Amin was thrown into prison despite his
personal relationship with President Nasser. His suffering in prison,
however, was our gain as he passed the tedious and painful days and
months in observing, thinking and writing. The result was a series of
letters later compiled in four books, each covering one year in gaol.
The material is most amusing and presents a damning indictment of
dictatorship, bureaucracy, terror, waste of talent and potential and
all that seems to go always with what is called paternal leadership,
guided democracy, people's democracy, etc. Yet the documents are

marred by the simple fact that Mustafa Amin is a humour columnist and not a political observer. Like al-Jahiz, who had said that he could not suppress a joke even if it led him to Hell, Mustafa Amin wrote that he could not resist a joke even when it meant his imprisonment. Reading his accounts of prison life under Nasser, all laced with endless jests and episodes, one simply cannot tell which is fact and which is fiction. Luckily, this present work is not an examination of prison conditions or totalitarianism, but a study in humour. The following is a sample piece.

Among the cases with me was a trumped-up case known as the case of the Arab Communist Party. The principal detainee was a man sentenced some seven years earlier for many forgeries. When he discovered that the government was giving the communists senior posts in the administration and the press ... he claimed that he was one of them. The communists, however, told him that he was only a forger, and in vain did he try to convince them that he had only done it to ruin the economy and thus win Egypt to communism.

A plan occured to me. He could deceive the Intelligence by posing as the chairman of a party called the Arab Communist Party, bent on staging a coup and making Egypt a communist state.

He fed such information to his brother-in-law who had contacts with the Intelligence. He thought that once the government heard of it, they would call him and give him a job at *Akhbar al-Yaum* for two hundred pounds a month. The Intelligence was pleased with this opportunity and arranged that he should allege that his intended coup was engineered by China. He was thus arrested and claimed that there were 120 people with him in the party. There were even unfounded confessions by some of them, although he was, in fact, the chairman, the rank and file and mass supporters all in one.

He told me with an astonishing frankness: 'Had I said that I was the only one in the party, no one would have paid any attention to me. But when I claimed that all these people were members with me and future ministers, I became an important personality.'

He was then asked to give them a list of the ministers who would form the government when the coup succeeded. He gave them the names of everyone who had done him harm in his life and decided to make them ministers.

He remembered Adli Abadir, the junior clerk at the Council of

Arts and Literature. The leader had once asked him to appoint him as an advisor to the Trade Union under the control of Abadir, but Abadir had apologized as the leader had not been a lawyer. He was punished for it now by being appointed as Minister of Culture. Abadir was arrested, beaten up and tortured until he confessed that he was the Minister of Culture of the coup. . .

The leader then remembered Muhammad Nasharti, the nurse at Qasr al-Ayni who refused to give him the address of a fellow nurse who owed him two pounds. He decided to punish Nasharti by appointing him as Minister of Health. They arrested Nasharti, tortured him and made him confess that he was the would-be Minister of Health. He then remembered his quarrel with Adil Sulayman, editor of *al-Jumhuriya*. Adil was appointed Minister of Information, arrested, beaten up, kicked about and tortured until he confessed that he was the Minister of Information. . . The leader remembered his sister, who was married to Sami Salam, a waiter at the Auberge, a Don Juan among the strippers and always betraying his wife. The leader decided that Salam should be punished for his adultery and had him appointed as Minister of Foreign Affairs. The waiter was arrested, beaten up, tortured and hanged from the ceiling until he confessed that he had agreed to be the future Minister of Foreign Affairs.

The state published in large headlines their success in arresting the members of the Arab Communist Party, whose leaders confessed to plotting a coup to seize power on behalf of China.[6]

All in all, Mustafa Amin wrote some nine thousand letters of this kind to his brother, Ahmad Amin, a feat which must have puzzled even his brother. But then the younger writer relates that the only way to keep him alive was to laugh all the way along, conjure up endless practical jokes and write these sheets and sheets of fun and satire. There is a wonderful description of the King of Torture and his pet dogs. The head of the prison establishment, Shams Badran, was annoyed with him and punished him by depriving him of the right to torture. 'Why? What crime did he commit to lose his monopoly of whipping and tormenting the prisoners?' He was forced to go on his knees to his boss: 'Please Shams Bey, for the sake of the Prophet . . . please, just let me torture this one young man.'

The King of Torture was entrusted with General Baysuni's four torture dogs, Rex, Golda, Inayat and Lacky. The general instructed that in deference to the honour of the bitch, Inayat, no amorous relationship should be allowed between Rex and Golda, a matter which was left as the responsibility of the prisoners. One night the entire prison was awakened by terrible barking and fighting. Inayat discovered her own Rex in a love scene with Golda, whereupon she protested against this public indecency on a public road, but the two lovers resented this blind jealousy and attacked Inayat. The poor bitch died cursing all the unfaithful dogs of husbands. A state of emergency was then declared in prison. General Baysuni came to receive the condolences of the officers and wardens who were all weeping for the untimely death of Inayat. Even the man who never shed a tear in sympathy for the scores of men whom he tortured and caused to die, cried for Inayat. 'Thank God for your luck,' said one warden to us, 'that the incident happened at night when you were in your cells.' General Baysuni then ordered one hundred strokes for each night warden and all the prisoners shouted, 'Long live justice.' Lacky then fell ill and went off his food and the doctor diagnosed old age and advised that he should be put down. The King of Torture had to perform the sad act, declare a state of mourning in the prison and weep bitterly for the passing away of this precious dog so skilful in biting and torturing the detainees. One of the wardens felt so upset that he ran amok and started to whip the prisoners. 'Cry! Cry, you sons of dogs. Your master, Lacky, has died.' '. . . And we all sat and cried for the dog who used to bite us.'

Thus Mustafa Amin remained cheerful by treating everything like a joke, including the plucking of his pubic hair and the pulling of his penis with a wire. The only occasion, so he says, on which they managed to make him cry was when they called his mother a whore. The world of the Arab is indeed a strange world. A man is not supposed to complain when they pull him by the genitals, but he should cry if they call his mother's genitals names!

However, the most hilarious letter in the collection was the one which he wrote to his brother on 27 February 1969. Mustafa Amin suffered from a combination of illnesses which made it difficult for him to use the primitive lavatory facilities arranged by the authorities. He had no choice but to buy his own portable lavatory and pay the younger prisoners cigarettes (the hard currency of prisons in the Middle East) to have it emptied. But he did not know what he was in for. The prison governor considered the piece quite out of order and confiscated it. Its owner had to apply to the highest authority in the land and use whatever influence he had to lift this prohibition.

Dear Brother, I am writing to you to send you my good wishes on this day of the *Id al-Adha* (the Muslim Feast of Sacrifice) and to give you, at the same time, a very good piece of news. Permission has been granted to use my portable lavatory. This was my great joy in this *Id*, almost like an *Id* present.

I have indeed received the loo which was imprisoned for three weeks at the governor's office. Whenever visitors called on him, they asked about it and he narrated to them the full story and told them that the piece was waiting for the order of release from the Minister of the Interior. I thank God that its case was not submitted to the Security Council and the durable deliberations of the four major powers, or to the forthcoming East–West summit conference. All these weeks I have been holding my breath lest a serious international crisis should happen and delay the restoration of the confiscated portable loo.

There was quite a demonstration when they brought it to me. Four soldiers preceded by the Staff Officer of the Liman Prison carried the lavatory shoulder-high like a political leader returning from exile, or like Mr Bhutto when released by the dictator Ayub Khan. I don't think that any portable lavatory used for urine and excrement anywhere in the world received this kind of honour and respect.

The lavatory was delivered to me at a formal reception at which I was asked to sign a document stating: 'I have received the pedestal lavatory for urine and excrement in accordance with the confidential letter of the Prisons Department of 25 February 1969, number 2902 marked SECRET 1462.'

I asked the officer whether the secret instructions stipulated that I should only use the lavatory in the presence of the Governor of the Liman Prison and the Chief Warden of the prison hall, or that I should have fresh permission from the Minister of the Interior every time I want to sit on it.

The officer replied that I needn't. But then he had second thoughts and promised that he would study the secret instructions and let me know.

I think I must be the only one in the republic who will use a pedestal loo with a letter classified SECRET from the Minister of the Interior, and bearing so many signatures. This is really a great honour, you know.

The prisoner went on to delve into the mysteries of political prisons:

The Governor of the Liman Prison is a naïve person and thought that the release of the pedestal lavatory is like the release of a sultan's throne. He intimated to the staff officers of the prison that it was not conceivable for the Minister of the Interior to release it without first consulting His Excellency, the Head of the State, as the use of the lavatory is an act of sovereignty. This permission of the President, therefore, implied presidential sympathy. The realists among the prisoners deemed the release of the loo as the beginning of indulgence. It would be followed by the release of the cigarettes which had been banned, and then the release of the pens and papers confiscated from us. It was further hoped that the newspapers, banished from the prison and obtainable only by smuggling in like narcotics, may also be allowed.

The pessimists, on the other hand, viewed the release of the loo with sinister foreboding. It meant that the portable lavatory was going to be the only prisoner receiving an amnesty on the occasion of the holy *Id*.[7]

Nevertheless, Mustafa Amin had occasions on which he stopped himself from laughing and looked at things more soberly with the result of some penetrating insight into the minds of prisoners sucked in by the problem of time and space:

A warden and an officer came yesterday and inspected my cell. The warden found my watch and fancied he had uncovered a grave violation. 'I found it,' he shouted to the officer, hurrying to him with the watch. The officer, however, replied calmly that watches were allowed by the authorities and mine was restored to me. Now my watch is as famous among the prisoners as the University Clock and the Cairo Station Clock. They rely on it for their prayers, their recreation, and for timing the closure of their cells.

Life without a watch is very painful. There were days which I spent without one. I used to try to find out the time by hanging on to the cell window and asking the gaolers. Sometimes they omitted the minutes. If it was five to seven, they told you it was six o'clock.

The time in which the the prisoners become unnerved is the few minutes before closing the cells. Every inmate tries to delay that action one minute or five minutes to enjoy freedom that bit longer. It is only the freedom of the hall, but things are relative here. They believe they are freer in the hall than in the cell. I try to convince them that there is no difference between the cell, the hall and the yard as long as they are all surrounded by prison walls. Peculiar how a prisoner feels free when he walks out of his cell or when he stays in but with the door open. He hates closed doors. He wishes to see his door open even when it only leads to another closed door or a series of closed doors.

In Mustafa Amin we clearly see how laughter is medicinal in many situations and for a variety of afflictions. That is why, perhaps, we see very few humorous characters among the medical practitioners who have other remedies to prescribe. Yet Iraq produced just this type of man. Maybe that was the result of the scarcity of drugs and medical care there. Almost every Iraqi worth the salt of his middle-class education can quote you one anecdote or another about Dr Faiq Shakir, the eye specialist of so many hats and guises.

Idiotic Third World bureaucracy put Dr Shakir in a Gilbert and Sullivan situation when Iraq was invited to attend an international seminar on psychiatry in Vienna and the government decided to send Faiq Shakir to represent the country. Upon his return, he described his participation in the seminar. He was made to sit next to a woman doctor from Finland. Halfway through the proceedings, she asked him what papers he had written recently and what discoveries he had made in this field of mental health.

'I am sorry; I am really only an optician!'

'Only an optician?' asked the mystified Finnish delegate.

'Yes. At least until I became Director of Supplies of the Iraqi Armed Forces.'

Dr Shakir noticed that the lady psychiatrist was getting even more puzzled, and so hastened to clarify his identity: 'But I was later on made Governor of the Province of Karkuk, in charge of our oilfields.'

'And what do you do now?' she asked.

'I am now the Mayor of Baghdad'.

The lady psychiatrist looked pale, fidgeted and then sent this hurried note to the chairman: 'Please help! The man next to me is an escaped lunatic.'

Dr Shakir's sense of humour, at least as related by his fellow countrymen, is copiously gingered with the usual obscenities of that land. When he was chairman of the board interviewing the new recruits to the Military College, a homosexual applicant appeared before him. He asked the young man the usual question of why he wanted to join the army. The recruit was too shrewd to mention the real reason that as an officer in Iraq he would receive twice the salary of a civilian, free land, a free car, a free loan, and almost a free wife. Instead he gave the board the stereotyped answer, 'I love my country and I want to defend it.' By then, Dr Shakir had had a good look at the confidential report on his homosexuality. 'Defend your country! Some two hundred thousand square miles from Mosul to Basrah, when you could not defend one square centimetre?' Middle Easteners find the anecdote not only witty but also a great piece of wisdom because, for them, a man may do all kinds of things without injuring his honour, as long as he does not become a passive gay.

On another occasion, acting as a general in the armed forces, he examined the case of a junior officer who appealed against the decision not to promote him to a higher rank. General Shakir looked closely at the young lieutenant – sturdy, fit and athletic. 'Tell me,' said the general to his officer, 'how is your sex instrument functioning these days?' The young man was taken aback and looked embarrassed and shy, but the general repeated the question and urged an answer.

'Well, sir, with the blessing of Allah, it is functioning all right.'

'So what is all this fuss about a higher rank?' said the ageing general. 'Give me your instrument, and take all these!' General Shakir grabbed his own stars, crowns and medals and flung them at the table in front of his lieutenant.

Like other Arab men of humour, Faiq Shakir made ample use of parables, which probably explains his popularity among the other politicians and public figures of Iraq. The one instance which has stuck in my mind all these years is the one involving the late Nuri al-Sa'id. The Prime Minister and most prominent leader of the royalist regime met Faiq Shakir at a reception and asked him for the latest in the country. Who is plotting, who is grumbling, what are they saying, and so on. Faiq Shakir was not a man to become an informer on his friends and parried the questions.

'What sort of Mayor of Baghdad are you,' said the Prime Minister, 'if you know nothing about what is going on in your city?'

'I am only a mayor and deal with politics indirectly. You are the Prime Minister. You should know. You deal with the people face to face. My example and yours is like that of the two lovers of Khirnabat'.

Nuri al-Sa'id became more intrigued and insisted that his mayor tell him the story and point to its moral.

'Once, in the remote village of Khirnabat,' said Mayor Shakir, 'a male teacher met a female teacher and the two fell in love. In that romantic mood, they decided to go for a country walk, which they did, cuddling and kissing. The conservative peasants were shocked. Where is it all going to end! Now the city *effendis* are bringing their decadence even to the country. To wash off this dishonour from this most religious and respectable village, the peasants attacked them and raped them both. The male teacher and the female teacher went to the police and the police, for once, acted with some efficiency and rounded up all the people sexually capable of the deed, which meant anyone between nine and ninety, for identification. All in dirty white *dishdashas*, dirty spotted *yashmaqs* and dusty thick moustaches, they all looked the same to these city dwellers. The male teacher and the female teacher looked and looked without ever coming to any definite idea.'

'Can't you tell, my dear,' said the female teacher at last to the male teacher. 'Can't you tell who they were?'

'I, tell!?' said the male teacher to the female teacher in absolute disgust. 'I was raped from behind. How can I recognize their faces? But you, my dear, you were ravished face to face. You should be able to know the faces of your ravishers.'

It is said that Nuri al-Sa'id was quite upset by the story and went on to report it to the Prince Regent, Abd al-Ilah, asking for the dismissal of this indecent mayor. The prince, however, laughed to his heart's content and could see no way to punish anyone who told this story.

All of the foregoing men of wit had Western education and a reasonable command of either French or English. Abd al-Aziz al-Bishri, the most renowned witty man in the modern Arab world, had none of that and was completely rooted in the tradition and learning of the old art of the classical *zarif*. Taha Hussein described him as one of the few rarities endowed with a light-hearted personality, sweet disposition and delicate qualities. A clergyman, theologian and a *qadi* or judge, he seems to have inherited from his father, who was also a shaykh and a *zarif*, his wit and inclination to humour, which was further nourished and sharpened by such renowned humourists and comics as Jamal al-Din al-Rumadi, Muhammad al-Bayli and Imam al-Abd, the man credited with the description of a butcher who took up journalism. 'He used to be followed by dogs. Now he is following the dogs.'

Like his father, he had tremendous presence of mind. He was once at a banquet when another *zarif* and friend of his wanted to tease him. Seeing al-Bishri's *jubba* (the cloak worn by Muslim clergy) hanging near the bathroom, he drew the image of an ass on it. Upon departure, al-Bishri saw this image on his *jubba* and shouted to the guests, 'Who has wiped his face on my jubba?' His *imma* (the large headgear worn by the clergy) was the source of another joke. An illiterate peasant stopped him in the street and asked him to read for him a letter. It was a mess of illegible scribbling and the shaykh could not make head nor tail of it, and could do no more than apologize for his inability to read it.

'What!' said the peasant, 'all this big *imma* on your head and you cannot read a small letter!'

Shaykh al-Bishri took off his *imma*, put it on the peasant's head and thrust the letter in his hands: 'There, now you read it!'

Al-Bishri was not a politician and did not involve himself in politics but his antics, jokes and remarks often carried *en passant* weighty political comments. With their rich history and proud culture, the Arabs often grumbled about the low calibre of the British administrators and advisers sent to manage their affairs and guide them in their development. Muhammad Hussein Haykal passed a poignant judgement on this situation. 'Every Englishman ... was seconded to Egypt for work for which he had neither the experience not the knowledge, but simply to get double his salary. It was sufficient that he was British to know all and perform all.' The result was a rule in which 'Equality in injustice was equal to justice.'[8] In that heyday of British imperialism, Aziz al-Bishri visited London and went to Piccadilly, where he had a shoeshine. When the job was finished, he gave the man a one-pound note and told him to keep the change. His friends were furious and told him that one shilling would have been sufficient. 'Hush!' he whispered to them, 'we had better stay on his good side. Two or three days and this shoeshine may be our next Inspector of Education.'

Many people compared the Shaykh al-Bishri with Bernard Shaw, but it may be more apt to compare him with al-Jahiz, who influenced al-Bishri to a great extent, as he had always influenced all other *zurafa'*. Al-Bishri's caricaturist portrayals leave no doubt about this influence, as in the picture he drew of Ahmad Ziwar, whose own style of humour, according to Sa'ad Zaghlul, made him more dangerous than Abd al-Khaliq Tharwat, because he did not arouse the anger of the people. 'He only activates in them their capacity for laughter and changes the serious into the frivolous. They don't dislike that. They may enjoy it.' Al-Bishri disliked Ziwar in person and in politics and went on to give him some of his own medicine:

The description and measurement of his external form, geometrical shapes, elevation plan and horizontal sections all
require skilful art and brilliant engineering. Once you look at this
man, you recognize immediately that he is composed of many
creatures joined together and clinging one to the other in a
manner which defeats your comprehension. You look and you
see that some of them are statics, others are motive! Some move
around themselves, others move around others. There are those
which are stiff and those which are fatty . . .

The people of Egypt accuse Ziwar as a 'whole' of countless
crimes against the national cause. They hold him guilty of
embezzlement of public funds and disregard to the interests of
the nation. But it is unjust to charge the innocent with the crime
of the guilty and unfair to punish the victim for the felony of the
delinquent. It may be that all those sins were committed by the
left elbow of Ahmad Ziwar, or the lower part of his abdomen or
the middle muscle of his right thigh . . . Justice and propriety
demand the formation of a commission of enquiry to investigate
with His Excellency and question his organs one by one and
examine him limb by limb. We shall probably find that one organ
is completely innocent of all that has been done, and that organ is
his brain. I do not believe that his brain played any part in
whatever he has done. . .

Ziwar also respects the hat [symbol of British and Western
influence for the Arabs] and would not deny any request to
anyone wearing a hat, so much so that it was said that some of our
great theologians, the sources of light and pillars of Islam –
having exhausted themselves, striving, trying and knocking at
every door in search of any vacant employment, decided in the
end to wear a hat, hoping to secure his sympathy and obtain some
estate or religious chair. Ziwar, our shaykh, finds no difficulty in
formulating a thousand religious *fatwas* justifying this usage.[9]

Another politician who irritated the shaykh was Dr Mahjub
Thabit, a jack-of-all-trades and master of none. He was once
entertained, together with Hafiz Ibrahim, the famous poet and
humorist, by Sa'ad Zaghlul, and the medical doctor started relating a
dream which he had. He dreamt he was riding a camel followed by
donkeys, when a man came and delivered to him a letter. Sa'ad asked
the poet whether he had any interpretation for the dream. Yes, it is
simple, said Hafiz. The camel is his seat in parliament. The letter is
the letter of his appointment as Minister of Health. The donkeys

behind him are the constituents who elected him to parliament. Shaykh al-Bishri had another way of dealing with the arrogant doctor:

> The doctor among the Egyptians is like England among the nations. They both think they bear responsibilities for the rest of humanity which will never be discharged to the end of time. If the subject was about the Nile . . . our doctor would take command of the discussion and silence all the engineers. If it was something to do with revolution, he would preside over the Central World Committee. Whenever there is a demonstration in town, Dr Thabit is its leader. Wherever there is a burial of a freedom's martyr, Dr Thabit is at the head of the funeral procession . . .
>
> Should the species of rats and squirrels and the families of lizards and cockroaches decide to organize themselves in a trade union, Dr Mahjub Thabit would be their orator and, with the blessing of the Almighty become their president.[10]

It was natural for Cairo Radio to tap the talent of the shaykh as soon as it commenced broadcasting in the thirties, and the shaykh's contributions proved to be sheer gems of Arab humour. His talk 'Death Insurance' still reads well – it is as fresh as when it was first given; after all, the problem which it treated has become even more critical and relevant than it was. The intrusion of the Western style of consumer society into the contented orient together with the competitive spirit of modern capitalism, aroused the expectations of the people and the ambitions and jealousies of the middle classes. The young man could no longer marry early, and a young woman would no longer accept Allah's kismet. Both began to live beyond their means and it became imperative for the young man to make sure of the extra income and windfall of his intended. The subject has become the theme of countless comedies, tragedies and novels as well as endless litigations and proceedings. The shaykh showed his sense of duty and talked about this problem:

> Young men's earnings, or resources as they are called nowadays, are no longer sufficient to meet the heavy demands of our time. Thus they are forced to give up all thought of marriage unless the wife has equivalent income or a rich father to whose death the young man can look forward. The advice here is that such a young man should first verify the extent of the assets of his

future father-in-law. Many men refuse to sign the marriage
certificate until they are shown all the deeds of the agricultural
lands, buildings and possessions. More diligent men go secretly
to the land registry to make sure that the immovable assets are
not burdened with any mortgage, charge, duty or other claims.
They then marry with a clear conscience.

But who can guarantee that God will soon end the life of such a
father-in-law? Many old men walked at the funerals of their
daughters and their daughter's children. It is therefore most
important that men should make sure not only of the validity of
the property deeds but also of the imminence of the owner's
death.

I knew a man, rich of assets, religion and dignity who had a
beautiful daughter, full of grace and learning. A civil servant
asked for her hand, and her mother dutifully showed him all the
land registration certificates and property deeds. Yet, he was not
satisfied and bribed a servant in the house to deliver to him all
the handkerchiefs used by the father. He almost frayed these
hankerchiefs with his close examination in search of any trace of
blood. But not everyone dies of TB and a specimen of urine may
have an additional advantage. Yet, how can you obtain such a
specimen without the knowledge of the father?

There is only one solution for this problem. A number of
insurance companies should be formed to insure against life. Just
like the existing life insurance policies, a young man intending to
get married may buy a death insurance policy, whereby the
insurer will pay the insured fixed monthly sums in the event of
the insured death of his rich father-in-law failing to materialize
within the specified period mentioned in the policy.

Once that is organized, men will be tempted into matrimony,
daughters will be married off, the idle will find employment and
the economy will pick up.

In another talk, he satirized the world of advertising by referring
to the bizarre Middle-Eastern habit of manufacturers publishing
their own personal photographs, instead of their products, in their
advertisements. 'Why not?' said the shaykh. 'Doesn't the Holy
Qur'an say, "we created man in the best form." God did not say that
about armchairs, beds or wardrobes.'

Writing about one of the cabinet ministers, al-Bishri touched on
the other endemic disease of the area – corruption and nepotism.

A friend and a member of the cabinet visited another minister one day and asked him to promote one of his lackey's on the understanding that he would reciprocate and promote a relative of the minister at his own bureau. The second minister used his big arithmetical brain in the computation of the deal and found that there would be a difference of forty piasters per month between the two promotions. The problem became intractable and in vain did they look for a solution. After lengthy negotiations and talks, a third minister who was present mediated in the matter and proposed that the second minister should increase the salary of a relative of the first minister employed in his own ministry by one hundred piasters, which was all that lay within his authority or power. After considerable persuasion the first minister accepted the deal allowing the balance of forty piasters as a monthly charity contribution to Allah.

Al-Bishri was only one in a distinguished gallery of great wits and elegant men of letters like Ibrahim al-Mazini, Fikri Abada, Ali Adham and Hafiz Ibrahim. It is one of the greatest losses for Arabic literature that Hafiz Ibrahim reflected almost none of his humour and light spirit in his grand social poetry, but the running battle of wits between him and al-Bishri should form an entire chapter in the literature of Arab humour. During a journey they were making together, Hafiz was late in the morning and al-Bishri had to wake him up quickly.

'Wait!' said Hafiz, 'I haven't washed my face yet.'

'No time to wash your face now. Just dust it,' said the shaykh.

But Hafiz soon got his own back. Seeing the poet approaching, the shaykh told him, 'Bless me! From a distance I thought you were a woman.'

Hafiz answered, 'It's old age. We are both losing our sight. I also saw you coming but I thought you were a man.'

The writer of the famous verse: 'Is the Azbakia Garden the abode of our sons and among the mosques is the sleeping abode of our old?' was as gentle and delicate as his companion, al-Bishri. Just think of his reply to the Khedive Abbas, the mean ruler who served indifferent meals. The khedive invited him once to dinner and asked him whether he had enjoyed it. 'Sir, I dined just as if I had dined in my own house.'

Shaykh Abd al-Aziz al-Bishri lived at a time when men of letters were comparatively free to lead at least their own lives according to their own fashion. A number of centres evolved in many Arab capitals where the litterateurs used to meet, crack jokes and discuss politics and Arabic grammer. In Baghdad, Café Swisse, Café Brazil and al-Zahawi Coffee House (which the famous poet Jamil al-Zahawi used to frequent), were the attraction of the élite. In Cairo, the Angelo Bar was the meeting place for such men of wit as al-Bishri, Ali Ibrahim and Fikri Abadha. Bar al-Liwa' and the Matatia Coffee House were no less famous among the learned and the eloquent. In Beirut and Damascus, the coffee houses of Ajram, al-Qazzaz and Brazil occupied a similar position. But soon a wind of change blew over the Middle East and men with guns stepped out of the shadows and looked back in anger. What they saw they did not like. The age of disillusionment set in and the sound of martial music replaced the melody.

Nabil Abu Hamad, *Iraq Monthly* 1981

5 The Age of the Cynic

> The joke was the devastating secret weapon which the
> Egyptians used against the invaders and occupiers. It was
> the valiant guerrilla who penetratad the palaces of the
> rulers and the bastions of the tyrants disrupting their
> repose and filling their heart with panic.
>
> Kamil al-Shinnaui

The Arab national revival was linked with the rise of Arab
nationalism which, in turn, was the product of the struggle against
the foreign occupiers, a struggle which was direct and clear, hinging
more on rhetoric, jingoism, patriotic poetry, grim discussions and
religious invocation. When humour was introduced, it was often in
the traditional form of parody. The most striking example was the
anecdote of *Mismar Juha* (Juha's Nail), which Fikri Abadha used
once in an editorial as a reply to the British offer of withdrawing
from the whole of Egypt and retaining only the Suez Canal Base. Ah,
said the Egyptian wit, this was going to be another nail of Juha, who
put his house up for sale with one condition – that one particular
nail in the house was excluded from the sale. A purchaser did not
think much of the condition and accepted it, but a few weeks later,
there was the knocking at the door. Juha wanted to assure himself
that his nail was all right. They had to let him in. Another stormy
night brought Juha to the door with his blanket. He wanted to make
sure that no harm would befall his nail, which he could only do by
sleeping by the side of his nail. Before the end of the year, Juha was
installed well and truly with bed, cooking stove and all, by his nail to
look after it. The old tale reverberated throughout the Arab world
and *Mismar Juha* entered the political vocabulary of the Arabs and
became the answer to any suggestion from the Western powers to
retain a presence in the Middle East. Ali Ahmad Baktir, a Hadramauti writer living in Cairo, dramatized this moral story in a play
which achieved great topical success. After 1945, Baktir was swept
along by the struggle for liberation and turned most of his attention

to the use of comedy as a political weapon. Britain received another attack from him in his play *Empire for Auction*. However, the earliest form of xenophobic literature was propagated by the comedian al-Rayhani, who used to ridicule the Turks by mocking their language and broken Arabic, a device which was also utilized by the dramatist, Mahmud Taymur, as well as many others.

But the attainment of independence released the contradictions which gave food to the satirists and cynics. The frustration of expectation, as Pascal had postulated, became impetus for laughter. The nationalist leaders believed and told their people that all their ills were due to imperialism and everything would be fine once they were free to do what they wanted. Very few of them had any idea of the intractable problems of a backward country groaning under the shackles of a glorious past. Naji al-Kishtainy, one of the early nationalist poets, related to me this true story which he considered as the first ill omen for the newly-gained independance of Iraq. Soon after the capture of Baghdad by General Maude, the British put a couple of military police on the riverside of the British residence to lash the backs of any boatmen daring to continue with the old custom of using the romantic Tigris River as a common sewer and the river bank of the British residence as a public convenience. British imperialism became a real thorn in the bladder of these poor boatmen. Iraq eventually managed to gain its independance and on the historical day of the Declaration, Mr Kishtainy, deputies and journalists dispersed from the Constitutional Assembly and went to the Risafa embankment to take the ferry boats to the Karkh. Amid the thundering of the guns and chanting of school children, the shrill voice of a boatman came from the direction of the British residence calling his mate on the other side, 'Hammad, Hammad! Come over and let's shit! We are independent now!'

Perhaps the most individualist people in the world, the 'prominent feature of the Arab character, today, as much as then, is their extreme turbulence and dislike of authority', General Glubb once wrote. But what aggravated the Arab observer more was the extreme inefficiency, corruption and stupidity of the new authority. Sabih Mumtaz, the Iraqi politician, was once approached by an applicant asking for a special favour.

'After all I have some rights in this government. I am one of the founders of this state,' said the man.

'Are you one of its founders?' asked Mumtaz, 'then bend down and let me take off my shoes! I have made an oath: if ever I find who founded this state, I must strike him with my shoe a hundred times on his head!'

East or West, the story is the same. Most Arab visitors were terribly disappointed when they visited Algeria, the Maghreb state of eighteen million people.

'Is this really the land of the one million martyrs?' asked an Arab from the Mashriq, referring to the number of Algerians killed in the war of liberation.

'No, brother!' said his Algerian host, 'this is the land of the seventeen million martyrs.'

Writing about the new independant state of Lebanon, Muhammad Abduh gave a prophetic picture:

I have never seen in my life a more intelligent and clever people than the people of Wardistan (Flower-land). They live under a unique political system based on religion. The president has his sect and the prime minister has another sect. Then all other posts, high and low, are distributed according to sect and religion. Thus the caravan goes on travelling in this exceptional order unbeknown to any other nation and unrivalled by any other land. In Wardistan, you find a group supporting Nifaqistan (Hypocrisy-land), another supporting Shiqaqistan (Dissension-land) and a third backing Tawritistan (Trouble-making-land). States finance all these groups to set up great press organizations publishing all kinds of books and magazines preaching the ideas of all these states which can also, as may be required, hire groups of people to demonstrate in the streets and cheer the state which pays for the demonstration. The conflict between the hirelings of the various states may occasionally develop into battles in which blood flows and the authorities intervene to halt the fighting and restore order. Out of this cleverness, unknown journalists achieve success and the hired contractors of the demonstrations and agents of the three embassies accumulate great wealth. Thanks to this ingenuity, prosperity is prevailing in Wardistan ...

It is the stock exchange of the area, dealing with ethics, commerce, light industries, newspapers, magazines and pirated books at the cheapest prices. It is an open import–export market, a land made for money and food. The *hors d'œuvre* consists of fifty or sixty dishes, each of which is a complete meal ...

This strange and bewildering country has no prototype in our universe. You wonder about the success of its political system with its religious and sectarian base. You wonder about the secret of its financial strength, with no rivers or raw materials. You wonder about its social stability although everything in it is based on contradictions. It has a budget without a balance sheet. It has streets with such traffic chaos that it looks like order. It has laws which operate outside the law. You then ask the citizens of Wardistan: 'How do you manage it with all these contradictions?' They give you one single answer: 'It's the freedom which our neighbours don't have.'

In a long and elegant letter addressed, in 1938, by Rose al-Youssef herself to the Egyptian Prime Minister, Ali Mahir Pasha, she piled on the defects of the national government and said,

What is the party life of Egypt other than a merrymaking and noisy crowd hustling behind a band? It is true, the people may sometimes get fed up with the tune because it is monotonous, but they still want it. They want something to follow and sing and drum to. The musicians are never tired of it and cannot anyway give it up because it is their first and last device, their only means of living and their only way of enjoying this leadership of the masses.

The formidable problems faced by the infant independent government were best illustrated by King Faisal in his introduction to al-Hasani's *History of Modern Iraq*, when he said that he had a government in possession of 15,000 rifles to rule over a people in possession of 120,000 rifles. The élitists, who had been to Europe and America, were too idealistic and impatient to remember that Rome was not built in a day, or appreciate the difficulty of converting a medieval, illiterate society into a modern nation. In one of the Baghdadi bars which I knew at the South Gate, three notices on the walls summed up the state of the nation:
'Singing is prohibited – by order of the Mayor of Baghdad.'
'Arms are not allowed – by order of the Military Governor.'
'Spitting is prohibited – by order of the Department of Health.'
Watching the bar for ten minutes, I saw the customers breaking all three orders within that brief time. In a visit to Cairo, I saw a tram carrying a much longer list of instructions, among which were the following:
'If a lady gets in, give her your place . . . but do not expect her to accept.'
'Do not spit on the tram. This is a sign of your ill-breeding.'

'Do not put your feet on the seat. You will soil it.'

'If you see women in front of you, do not molest them with your looks and gestures.'

There is a class structure within the twenty-three Arab states in which the Lebanese ridicule the Syrians who ridicule the Iraqis who ridicule the Saudis and the Gulf people. The Egyptians ridicule the Sudanese who ridicule the Somalis, and all ridicule the Yemen as the most backward land in the world, so much so that God recognized it. They said that Allah once asked Gabriel to show him what had happened to earth, and the angel started with America – the skyscrapers, Disneyland, Hollywood ... etc. 'This is America,' said Gabriel and God was overwhelmed with wonder. Then he showed him England – all the defunct railway lines, abandoned collieries and idle industries and dockyards. 'This is England' and God was overwhelmed with even more wonder. The tour went on until they reached South Arabia and God said, 'Oh, yes. I know this place. It is the Yemen. Just as I made it.'

Many stories were circulated about the monarchy of what was called 'The Happy Land of the Arabs', in view of its great ancient civilization. The king was usually projected as a man devoted to modern technology, to which he allocated the best room in his palace, where he set up a giant toy railway. Another acquisition was the tape-recorder which he ordered as soon as he heard of it. He had the microphone secretly installed in the state hall. During cabinet discussions, he would get up and go inside to play with his trains, leaving the tape-recorder secretly on. By the end of the day, and having listened secretly to the recordings, he would go back and tell each minister what he had been saying. The ministers would then all kneel in awe and wonder. The king is truly God's shadow on earth endowed with the gift of knowing the unknown.

Against the background of such mythology, Abdulla al-Sallal toppled the monarchy and established a republic, only to face the same frustration. While in Cairo for medical treatment, he fell into the hands of Egypt's wits. They said that he was suffering from piles; that he went to Qasr al-Ayni, that a specialist prescribed electric treatment. Coming out of the first session, the President of the Yemen said, 'The electric power entered my arse and has not yet entered the Yemen.' The squalor of the country struck many visitors, including Field Marshal Abd al-Hakim Amir, who whispered in the president's ear the importance of hygiene and public decency. The president replied that such things happen everywhere. On his next visit to Cairo, he actually saw a man urinating in the airport gardens. 'There! You have similar scenes here.' Amir was furious and sent the police to arrest the offender. When the man was brought before them, they discovered he was the Yemeni Ambassador.

Many Arabs may be offended by hearing such stories, but this objection is itself part of the comic situation, i.e. the inability to come to terms with the facts of life and narrow the gap between the conception and reality, the reality of centuries of backwardness, poverty and neglect. But then, the proud Arabs do not like admitting any shortcomings and the Iraqis have a good proverb which they often cite in describing their condition. A tribesman from Shammar was asked the usual question about his people. 'Oh Shammar is well and prosperous and in need of nothing other than food and clothes!' One of the problems which frustrated the efforts of the politicians and reformers is the long and proud history of the area and its old culture, which makes it impregnable to any call for change. Both the Christian missionaries and the communists suffered a great deal on this score. One missionary made some exceptional efforts with which, in the end, he could win a handful of converts. During an area visit by his bishop he wanted to exhibit his success and present his flock. In a sermon carefully rehearsed for the occasion, he went on to relate the miracles of Christ and started by the raising of Lazarus. No sooner did he finish his story than the whole congregation of converts chanted in one voice, 'Oh, praise be to Muhammad.'

The whole Arab national movement is the work of the middle class, or what is more precisely described as the educated class (*al-tabaqa al-muthaqqafa*) and the sons of this class expected their due reward. Arabs do not like manual labour or work associated with manual labour, and the inherited respect and fear their fathers had held for the foreign rulers and officials made the civil service a coveted aim, especially under the circumstances of corruption. Everyone wanted to be a 'Gov' and the inflated bureaucracy lay heavily on the bosom of the people with rows and rows of clerks, supervisors and inspectors with nothing to do other than put a stamp on papers which they never read. A castrated man won a place among all these rows and his new boss told him, at the interview, to commence work the following day at twelve o'clock.

'Why twelve o'clock sir? Office hours begin at nine.'

'Yes', said the boss, 'all employees come at nine, but until twelve, they do nothing but play with their balls. You have no balls – so why come early?'

In 1977, the Iraqi press reported the scandal of the lone cyclist who was sent to participate in the Asian sports competition in

Bangkok with twelve bureaucrats to look after him, and he brought up the rear. The news editors were very scathing about the episode and with good reason, for none of them was invited to accompany him.

The over-staffed Arab League, where unwanted politicians are usually dumped by their governments, represents all that is worst in the Arab World, and Haykal had no other words to describe it than to say that it was 'a joke hurtful to anything Arab'. A friend working there described the atmosphere: 'When you visit us you will find us all asleep, but suddenly one day you may find great hustle and bustle and people rushing with files in every direction. That means there is a delegation going somewhere to defend the Arab case, and everybody is trying to have his name included. Once the list is finalized, the hustle dies with the same speed and everybody goes back to sleep.' In 1966, Mr Hassuna, the Secretary General, had a similar flash of humour about its work. If only the war in the Yemen ended, he said, the Egyptian–Syrian relations were sorted out, the internal situation in Syria was normalized, a rapprochement was made between Saudi Arabia and Egypt, the enmity between Egypt and Jordan was contained, the frontier dispute between Morocco and Algeria was solved, tranquillity was restored to the south and north of the Sudan, and Tunisia paid more attention to Arab issues, the Arab states would enter a golden age.[2]

After Sadat's visit to Jerusalem the Arab League was shifted to Tunisia and the Tunisians seem to have treated the move as a great winner for the tourist industry. A young Tunisian was seen sitting outside the Arab League offices with a trumpet in his lap. A friend saw him in that bizarre posture and wondered what he was doing. 'What are you doing with this trumpet?'

'This is my new job,' replied the man, 'to wait for Arab unity and then declare it to the world with this trumpet when it is established. I get fifty dollars a month for it.'

'This is a very miserable salary,' said the other.

'Yes, but remember this is a lifetime job.'

Under the heading of 'In honour of the State of Bureaucrats', the Lebanese journalist, Adil Malik, described his country's productivity. The year for the government is 365 days, less fifty-two days' Christian weekends, less fifty-two days' Muslim weekends, less thirty days' state holidays, less twenty days' annual leave, less twenty days' sick leave. The balance is 191 days in which no citizen is allowed into any office before eleven in the morning or after midday.[3]

One assumes that those insignifant bureaucrats have little influence on people's life, but the fact is that everybody spends a sleepless night before calling on their offices. After all, the rubber stamp can be lost, broken, locked in the safe, the accountant having forgotten the code ... You may well hear of a mother talking proudly of her daughter's fiancé, 'He is a Grade VI clerk at £20 a month but he also earns £80 in bribes.' Writing of the sway which the bureaucracy held over the country, Muhammad al-Tabi'i said:

> Show me a country like Egypt in which no minister has a cold or headache without all the newspapers reporting the cold or the headache with prayer to the Almighty, the Healer and Curer of all to speed the recovery of the indisposed minister! Show me a country like Egypt in which no civil servant takes a holiday without the press wishing him a safe journey and comfortable stay and praying that he may return to resume his work with the same energy and devotion known of him. Show me a country like Egypt in which no civil servant dies without the press mentioning that the hand of death picks up only the precious jewels. Show me a country like Egypt in which no civil servant is tranferred from town to town without the press reporting that he is leaving behind souls deep in love and esteem for him on account of his great devotion, justice, fairness and high morals ... [4]

There is a parable which illustrates the deep love and esteem felt by the poor souls for their bureaucrats. When the horse of a governor died, the whole town walked at its funeral, but when the governor died no one walked behind his coffin. The joke which I heard from nationals of many Arab countries was the one about the government of shit. A man was arrested for shouting in the streets, 'Government of shit.' At his trial, the judge asked whether the police report was true.

'Yes, I did say that, but I didn't say "our government". Maybe I had the Turkish government in mind or the Soviet government or ...'

The judge then turned to the officer: 'Yes. What made you think he meant our government?'

'Sir,' said the police officer, 'there is no government of shit in the world other than our government.'

This man was lucky to have an attentive judge, for other anecdotes inform us that judges never listen during the hearing. A pupil was once asked by his teacher, 'Is sleeping sickness confined to Africa?'

'No, sir. The judges of our mixed courts also suffer from it.'

In a true story, a defence counsel noticed that members of the court were whispering to each other. So he stopped his submission to give them a chance to sort out the point.

'You go on with your defence,' said the president of the court to the counsel. 'We are talking about something else.'

Most probably about their dinner.

This is a subject with a very rich harvest in which the real is mixed with the invented and the funny with the tragic, and the listener is often at a loss as to which is which. Is it fiction, for example, that an unqualified and ignorant teacher went to his uncle, the minister, and informed him of the decision to set all teachers an examination, which he was bound to fail? The minister said, 'Well, the only way out is to appoint you as Chairman of the Examination Board.' Or is it true that a representative of a foreign company was approached by a chief engineer in Morocco to give a thousand dollars for an award of a contract? The representative reported the approach to the minister and the minister was furious. The engineer had no right to award any contract. 'Give me two thousand, and I'll sack him and give you the contract,' said the indignant minister.

The representative went and related the story to a member of parliament. 'Scandalous!' said the MP, 'this is no way to run our affairs. The minister has no right. Give me five thousand and we'll bring down the government and award you the contract.'

The representative went to the prime minister and told him everything. 'This is unbearable! This is unconstitutional interference. Give me ten thousand and I'll have this parliament dissolved and hold new elections and give you the contract.'

Against all this nagging and scandal-mongering, the authorities could think of nothing other than suppression, and a series of regulations, legislation and military orders were issued banning even the most harmless grumble. Serving time in prison became part of a journalist's life, so much so that in Egypt a complete new career was created in the thirties known as 'the Prison Editor' – a man who did not own the magazine, edit it, write in it, or do anything for it. His only function was to have his name printed as the 'responsible editor' and to go to prison whenever this responibility was in question, thereby allowing the real editor and staff to continue with their work. Maruf al-Risafi, Iraq's great social poet, wrote a famous eulogy for the freedom of expression:

> Speak not, O people,

For talking is prohibited.
Sleep and never wake up,
Only the sleeping win.
Regress from anything,
Which beckons to progress.
Give up trying to understand
Better for you, not to.
Hold on to your ignorance,
It is evil to learn.
Laugh, when you suffer injustice,
Be merry and never complain.
Thank them when they insult you
And smile when then they strike your face.
If they say your honey is bitter
Say 'Like colocynth!'
If they say your day is night
Say 'And how dark!'
If they say your puddle is a torrent
Say 'And flowing fast!'
And if they say O people,
Your country will be partitioned
Praise them, thank them,
Swing and sing.

Jokes about censorship, official or editorial, are common in all countries, but in the Middle East they become jokes of the absurd. Even the annual commemoration of the seventh-century martyrdom of Imam Hussein was viewed with suspicion by the authorities. A young clerical shaykh was briefed by the police in Bahrain on what to say and what not to say. He was not to mention that the Umayyads killed the Imam lest the Syrians should take offence; nor the Sunnis and Shi'is as this might weaken the national unity; nor the Christians who might consider it as discrimination; nor the Jews as the Zionist might treat it as anti-Semitism. He must not mention what he died for or how he was butchered ... etc. The shaykh turned to the governor: 'Can I say he touched an electric cable and died?'

A more authentic story actually happened to me when I represented the Arab League's magazine *Arab Affairs*. My brief was that contributors should have absolute freedom to write anything they liked about the Arab World provided that they did not criticize or offend any of the twenty-three Arab states.

The suppression of opinion inspired a variety of jokes on the theme of the 'shut mouths' of the public. Mrs Sadat was shopping in one of Cairo's luxury shops when the shop assistant broke wind. 'How dare you!' said the first lady of Egypt. 'Madam,' replied the assistant, 'Your husband shut our mouths. You want now to shut our arses?'

The successive regimes of Iraq proved to be some of the most allergic to any expression of personal opinion. On his way back from a medical conference in London, Dr Qutaiba al-Shaykh Nuri related that he was asked during the conference whether Iraqi doctors had added anything new to the great medical legacy of their ancestors. Oh, yes, he told them. They invented recently a robot which could be guided from the bottom, along the intestines, through the stomach, up the gullet and then to the throat to remove the infected tonsils electronically.

'Fine,' said the listener, 'but why all this way around? Why don't you use it directly through the mouth?'

'But who dares open his mouth in Iraq?' said Dr Nuri.

One man forgot, however, and opened his mouth at the conference of his political party. After delivering his long report to the meeting, the secretary of the party asked whether anyone had any question. Comrade Abbas stood up and after praising all the great achievements of the revolution, he added that there was only one point he wanted to raise – the question of the potatoes. They had completely disappeared from the market. The secretary promised to look into the matter. At the next meeting of the party, the same ritual was repeated as usual, and another comrade stood up, praised the achievements of the revolution and asked his question: 'It is really only a small matter. What happened to Comrade Abbas? He has completely disappeared.'

This joke is imported from Russia and acquired great popularity in Iraq, but the following one, which gained its own popularity in Syria, seems to be imported from the West. Four officers from America, Russia, Britain and Syria found themselves in Africa, and decided to make a bet on bringing a monkey from the jungle. The American used his electronic devices, located a monkey and brought it out in an hour. The Russian contacted the local comrades who led him to a monkey which he produced in two hours. The British contacted Scotland Yard and came out with a monkey in three hours. The Syrian officer then went in and three days passed without any sign of him. The three others went to look for him and found him beating up a zebra tied to a tree, and shouting at it: 'Admit you are a monkey!'

More oriental in spirit is the next anecdote about the man who
was making his new-year prayer. On sighting the crescent of the new
lunar year, he held his money and changed it from one hand to the
other, as customary, with the prayer: 'O, God, changer of all things,
change our state into another.'

A friend interrupted the ritual. 'This is not how the prayer goes.
Not into another but into a better.'

The old man replied, 'Into another is good enough for us. Things
can't get any worse.'

Many stories were circulated about Gadaffi's African missionary
exploits. An African leader who was persuaded to embrace Islam
asked him about the ritual of entering Islam and the Libyan leader
informed him of the act of circumcision.

'And what will you do if the man reverts from Islam?'

'We cut off his head,' said Gadaffi.

'This is a strange religion which cuts off one's penis on entering it
and one's head on leaving it!'

In a similar story another African leader was tempted by funds to
enter Islam, but he kept none of his pledges to Gadaffi, whereupon a
refund was demanded of him. 'Restore my penis, I restore your
money,' was the logical reply.

How can we decribe the style of the modern Arab satirist? In
addition to the bulk of westernized jokes, jibes and anecdotes, either
completely imported and arabized from the West and Eastern
Europe, or produced under the influence of Western education, the
old forms continue in evidence. The verbal and Qur'anic jokes
remain as popular – so do sex jokes, smut and parables. Female
emancipation and the free discourse between men and women have
brought the female sex and the wives and relatives of political
opponents into the firing line more than ever before. One queen was
particularly vilified with numerous jokes about her promiscuity. As
she sat with crossed legs one day, one of her legs said to the other,
'Goodness! Haven't seen you for ages!' The wife of another head of
state was accused of similar promiscuity. Tired of the political
frustrations of his country, her husband opened his heart to her and
went on reminiscing about the good old days when they were both
young and courting in the romantic haunts of the lovers' lanes. His
wife sympathized, responded and pulled him to her – 'Let us go and
relive the old times.' They took the car and went incognito to the
same nocturnal scenes. Refreshed by their mood, they made love –
and were spotted by a policeman. The leader begged him to let them

go. 'Never mind you,' said the officer, 'you can go. But this whore – I know her well. She comes here every night and does it with different men.'

Nothing can equal the disgrace of a woman indulging in illicit sex except the disgrace of a man unable to. Thus critics spread the rumour that a certain leader had lost the ability to perform and was indeed reduced to oral sex only. Another leader who did not like the statements made by his opposite number went on to say, 'If only our brother would put his tongue to a better use, how much more the Arab nation would have benefited!' It is interesting to note as a measure of the Arab's deep respect for Nasser that, despite the mass of jokes and jibes about him, none of his critics stooped to include him or his household in this familiar quagmire of obscenities. Wits always have sharp eyes and know where to hunt.

Less cruel people confined themselves to the old parables and moral fables of animals. A fable based on the sex life of beasts was related by Abd al-Qadir al-Barrak, a notable Iraqi journalist with solid political commitments. In his later days, however, he wrote some untypical editorials flattering the existing regime, for which, and for stooping to the level of the rest of the hack journalists, he was criticized. In his happy land of one thousand and one wonders, the peasants follow the ancient practice of procuration by putting all the bulls on one side of the field and all cows on the other with a strong fence between them for a number of days to increase their eagerness. The excited bulls roar, hit the ground with their hooves, charge at the fence and do all kinds of mad things. The owner of the farm was surprised to see a castrated bull among them doing the same, and with even more enthusiasm. 'Why are you doing that, castrated as you are?' enquired the farmer, and the bull replied, and Mr Barrak reported, 'If I don't do as they are doing, they'll see that I have no balls and I'll be ravished by all of them.'

Another fable was made up by a fellow journalist. A rabbit could no longer endure the famine of the country and heard of the bear who was doing well in the circus. So he went to see him, and was kindly received by him.

'Hello, little rabbit,' said the bear.

'Rabbit!' protested the pretty little thing, 'I am a bear. You are a rabbit.'

The joke became serious and turned into an argument, and the two animals contested the case in court. The lions who sat in judgement demanded certificates. 'Everything in this country must be proven by papers.'

The poor bear was not prepared for this and could produce nothing, whereas the clever rabbit instantly submitted his certificate, duly taxed and stamped under the emblem of the immortal republic testifying that he was a bear. The lions had no option but to give a verdict in favour of the rabbit who then took the place of the real bear in the circus. The dejected bear went on roaming the land where he discovered that the lions who sat in court were no lions at all, only donkeys certified as lions.

The story, however, has another moral. When it was first submitted, the editor became apprehensive lest the ministers of the government should recognize themselves in the animal characters. To mitigate the problem, he changed the word 'donkeys' to 'mules'. It seems that the editor was also operating with a false certificate!

It seems that the people of the East are determined to abuse the poor donkeys in fiction as well as in real life, for in the next story it is also this peaceful and hard-working animal which is libelled. For a very long time the only statue in the streets of Baghdad was that of Muhsin al-Sa'dun. Prime Minister Tahir Yahya stopped on his way as he saw the statue crying. 'I am tired of standing,' said the statue. 'All other heroes in the world have horses and sit in comfort and dignity. Only here, you treat your heroes thus.' Tahir Yahya was touched and promised to bring him a horse, and went forthwith to President Abd al-Salam Arif to report what he had seen. Arif ridiculed the report and Yahya offered to take him to the statue and let him see for himself. As the two leaders approached the plinth, the statue turned to Tahir Yahya admonishingly, 'You promised to bring me a horse, not an ass.'

Michel Aflaq, founder of the Ba'ath Pan-Arab Socialist Party, puzzled many religiously minded Muslim opponents of the Ba'ath with his inter-denominational approach to religion, his attitude to Islam and leadership of Muslim masses despite his Christian faith. His opponents could not but recall the story of the stork who soiled the church bell with his droppings every day. The unhappy priest consulted his bishop about the problem. 'You must pray to this stork to make him go elsewhere,' said the bishop. But before doing that the priest was instructed to find the religion of the stork. To test whether he was Muslim, he put next to the bell a glass of *arak*. The following day the *arak* was gone. The second test was to see whether he was a Jew, and a piece of pork was put for the purpose. The next day, the piece of pork was gone and the next Sunday the church bell was soiled again. The exasperated priest went up to him. 'For Heaven's sake, tell me! You are not Muslim because you drank *arak*.

You are not a Jew because you ate pork. You are not a Christian because you leave all this vast country and come here to shit on our church bell. In God's name, tell me, what is your religion?'

Perhaps the disillusionment was given an eloquent expression in the words of the old sergeant major who arrived at London Airport for medical treatment with half of his bones crushed by a series of civil wars and glorious misadventures. As he leaned on his crutches, looking at the Union Jack fluttering over the building, he moaned, 'Oh, wicked imperialism! Why did you leave us?'

Mahmud Kahil, *Al-Sharq al-Awsat* 1983 and 1985

6 The Golden Age of Nasser

> Because of his awesome presence, the king is insulted in his absence.
>
> Egyptian proverb

The reader must be gradually gaining the impression that Egypt is the unrivalled home of Arab humour, something which is indeed conceded by all Arabs – but one can go even further. Speaking from personal impressions, I can hardly think of any people who are so engrossed in humour and treat life like a laughing matter, as the Egyptians – almost to the point of aggravation. Turning any momentous question to a joke and any serious statement to a trifling rhyme or pun can be very vexing to most people. An Egyptian would leave his wife, children and comfortable home and go out to crack jokes and listen to jokes in a dingy café with the same enthusiasm and ruthlessness with which an Englishman leaves his family and his work to watch a football match. The humorous writer, Ibrahim Abduh, described his people like this: 'They are the laughing, smiling and cheerful people, the merriest of all peoples ... For thousands of years they survived with half of the working men dropping dead with hunger and cold while the other half cracked jokes and jibes. Sometimes, the jokes and jibes were more powerful than bullets.'[1]

One cannot be sure about the last word, but the jokes and jibes might have been, indeed, the secret behind the Egyptian's knack of survival. Egypt's record of humour extends far beyond any nation's memory as evidenced in the colossal caricature statues adorning now the entrance to the Louvre. There is always a smirk on the face of Egypt's gods, a smile on its statues and a built-in joke in its works of art, holy or profane. The little figures walking in the endless sacred processions to the netherworld, walk as if with a sense of comedy. What is even more telling about the character of this nation is its ancient belief that the world was created through a

series of laughs from the God. Out of the first laugh, the seven parts
of the universe emerged. With the second laugh there was light, and
with the third laugh there was water. The soul was finally created
with the seventh laugh.[2] It is further said that the Romans
prohibited the Egyptians from the practice of law at the courts of
Alexandria because they found the jokes and playfulness of the
Egyptian advocates detrimental to the respect of law. Centuries
later, Muslim travellers and scholars recorded similar impressions
as was mentioned, for example, by Ibn Khaldun in his Prolegomenon
when he described the Egyptians as a people of mirth, joy, light-
heartedness and inadvertence.

What made the inhabitants of the Nile valley such funny people
is anybody's conjecture, but mine is based on the same concept of
escapism, or 'the anaesthesia of the heart', as Bergson put it. The
Egyptians' reliance on irrigated agriculture along a very narrow strip
of a single river subjugated them both to the land and the overlord
who ruled over it. It was an agriculture which required many hands,
and consequently a high birth rate, in return for a poor, disease-
ridden and tragic living. Surrounded by desert and sea, there was no
escape from this narrow plot of land. Until very recent years, this
landbound society did not take to emigration as other Mediterranean
nations have done. Some form of mental escapism must be found to
alleviate this inescapable situation and the Egyptian found it in the
strong belief in the hereafter, in drug addiction and in humour.
Abbas Mahmud al-Aqqad summed it up in a few words: 'Jest and
religiosity are the twins of Egyptian character.' For a practical
example, we may recall how Mustafa Amin passed the painful hours
of his imprisonment under Nasser in an unbroken chain of jokes
and invocations of the name of God. As indifference is the natural
environment for laughter, laughter is the mother of indifference.[3]

Nowhere can we appreciate the essence and function of the
Egyptian sense of humour more than in Cairo's famous buses and
trams, which are the quintessence of Egypt's life, with its human
congestion, noise, squalor, fatalism and bondage. With any other
people in a similar hot climate, the bus stops would witness daily
shooting scenes – but not in Cairo.

'If you don't get out of this bus, I'll not move,' said the driver to a
man struggling to get in through the window, his head and shoulders
buried in a passenger's lap and his legs kicking desperately outside
the window. 'If I don't get in, you won't move,' answered the man. 'I
am the conductor.'

Everybody laughed and the sixty or probably one hundred

passengers shouted in one refrain, *Salli a'l Nabi* (Prayer for the Prophet). Cairo's public transport does not depend on petrol or power as much as it depends on the two magical words of '*Salli a'l Nabi*' which combines so eloquently Egypt's two elements: humour and religiosity.

Among this people emerged Jamal Abd al-Nasser as the compassionate patriot leading the Arab nation to freedom, dignity, prosperity and socialism, but fulfilment fell far short of the promises, and with that frustration of expectation, to borrow Pascal's words, the scene was set for a glorious time of verbal fun. Although no great wit by any standard and often intolerant of any criticism or dissension, Nasser enjoyed his country's national sport of exchanging jokes. He was reported to have insisted on a daily brief of the latest current jokes about him and his regime. Mustafa Amin, who had personal dealings with him and was his friend and confidant at one time, put it this way: 'Abd al-Nasser was sensitive to criticism. He would tolerate what you said against his actions when you were alone with him but woe to you if you repeated the same in front of strangers, even if they were the closest people to him.' When no one else was within hearing, he laughed heartily as Mr Amin compared the president's associates with the lion's riders who frighten everyone with the lion when they are most frightened by it.[4]

Nasser was conscious and respectful of his people's predilection for humour and appreciated their cheerful spirit. When Yusif al-Siba'i returned from a visit to China, and described to him the sacrifice and hard work given by the Chinese people for the sake of building up their country, Nasser was not impressed and had only this comment to make:

> When I remember the building worker carrying the load of mortar on his shoulder and climbing the scaffolding, singing his merry song, I feel that no one has the right to silence his song or wipe out his smile. I am no supporter of sacrificing one generation for another ... We are a people who laugh and work, who sing and work. I don't think that there is anything which can justify the suppression of a man's laughter and song.[5]

Although he was not a particularly witty politician, there is sufficient material to indicate a potential in that direction.

Sir Anthony Nutting, who knew Nasser well and became his personal friend, found him a man whose sense of humour had never deserted him. In his biography of the Egyptian leader, he relates how his fountain pen had run out of ink and he had to borrow Nasser's pen to sign the new treaty with Egypt. But in the excitement of the ceremony, Sir Anthony put the fountain pen inadvertently in his own pocket. Nasser held out his hand and with a broad grin said, 'I think you have already got enough out of me in this treaty. Please can I have my pen back,'[6] It is interesting to note that the comic dramatist Tawfiq al-Hakim was Nasser's favourite Arab writer and Voltaire was his favourite European writer about whom he had written in his youth an article for his school magazine.[7]

In another anecdote related by Siba'i, Nasser's family gave a birthday party for him for the first time – realizing, I suppose, that a head of state must have a birthday and a birthday party. As they asked him to blow out the candles on his cake, the president looked bashful, but managed to say pointedly,' I have never put out any candle in my life.' Dealing with the possible economic pressures and sanctions against Egypt, he shrugged them off with the words, 'Our people can do without soap for a whole year.'

Like all totalitarian leaders, he was obsessed with security and spying on his friends and foes alike, which resulted one day in a bizarre tape, recorded by his agents, of one of his ministers having sex with a mistress. The man had to go but Nasser kept the recording and kept on playing it as an exceptionally rare joke. Tape-recording was just coming into common use and the fashion seems to have fascinated him and inspired him to record his own conversations. He once told the American Ambassador that he had something very confidential which he wanted to discuss with him. He led him out into the garden for that exchange, but as it was pouring with rain the ambassador could not understand why they should suffer the wrath of nature when they could do the talking comfortably inside. 'The tape-recording is going on there,' answered Nasser, 'and I don't know how to stop it.'

In his early encounter with Colonel Gadaffi, the over-enthusiastic leader of Libya harangued him with his plans and designs for the Arab nation, but Nasser tenderly replied, 'You remind me of my youth.' The Libyan Information Department printed the words in all sorts of colours and hung them throughout Libya. Gadaffi was one of the millions of Arabs who simply worshipped Nasser and battled against the remaining millions who hated Nasser. Imam Ali's words, 'There will come a time in which people will hate me to the point of blasphemy and other people will love me to the point of blasphemy,' applied with the same degree of truth to the Egyptian leader. In

Qasim's prisons, the other leader of the coup, Abd al-Salam Arif, met the former Prime Minister of Iraq, Dr Fadhil al-Jamali, and asked him: 'What has brought you here?'

Dr Jamali replied, 'I stood against Nasser. And what has brought you here with me?'

'I stood for Nasser,' replied Arif.

The main factor in creating this crazy situation was Nasser's ambition to force Arab unity under the hegemony of Cairo and impose his will on other leaders. On one of the Muslim holy days, the leaders of the Muslim world were taken to Heaven and were introduced to God by the Archangel Gabriel. Every time a leader was presented, God rose from his throne and welcomed him, but when Nasser's turn came, God remained seated, and the Archangel added a few more words in God's ears and wondered why He did not rise to welcome this great champion of Islam and Arabism. 'I am afraid he may take my place on the throne,' God said.

In another story, King Hussein came out of the Mosque of the Rock and was mobbed by the beggars. 'Give us some of what God has given you,' said one, and the King gave him one fils. 'Give us some of what the King of Iraq has given you,' said another and Hussein gave him one dinar. 'Give us some of what the King of Saudi Arabia has given you,' said a third and Hussein gave him a golden sovereign. 'Give us some of what President Nasser has given you,' said the fourth and the King gave the *khazuq* (the equivalent of the rude two fingers sign).

Nasser was well aware of all these jokes and it is said that he was once rather badly irked by one jester who kept on producing these unflattering anecdotes. The president finally asked for the man to be brought before him and started to censure him and remind him of all his achievements and popularity '. . . and remember I was elected by ninety-nine per cent of the electorate,' said Nasser.

'I swear,' rejoined the man, 'this was not one of my jokes.'

Of course, the pretence to democracy and free elections was undoubtedly a joke and the Syrians, who had a democratic and parliamentary system before joining Egypt in unity, had a great deal to say about it. As the Syrian deputies entered the parliament of the United Arab Republic in Cairo, they found two doors before them, bearing these words: 'Deputies of the Northern Region' and 'Deputies of the Southern Region'. They entered the first one and found two more doors, 'Appointed Deputies' and 'Elected Deputies'. They entered the latter door and found two more doors, 'Deputies with questions to ask' and 'Deputies with no questions'. They entered the first and found the security police waiting for them.

It is the secret police and its raids of terror, torture and arbitrary detention which come always first on the lips of Nasser's critics in their indictment of his regime, under which all forms of free expression and discussion were ruthlessly suppressed. They tell you that dogs in Libya were stunned (before the discovery of oil) by the sight of an Egyptian dog running furiously towards their border. 'What are you coming here for?' they said to him, 'we are all starving.'

'I want to bark,' said the dog from Egypt.

Only flattery was allowed and rewarded and the result of the competitive spirit in this flattery broke beyond any reason among the press reporters. In celebrating the first anniversary of the revolution, one of the newspapers estimated the number of the demonstrators filling a Cairo square as half a million people. Another newspaper said it was more than one million and a third newspaper put the figure at one million and a half. 'Had there been ten newspapers in Nifaqistan [Hypocrisy-Land], the number of demonstrators would have reached five million,' wrote Ibrahim Abduh.

One reporter described the visit of the president to a desert farm and said that the hens were flying in joy at his visit.[8]

Once you are in the street you have to join the common chorus of praise: Long live the champion of Arab unity! Long live the vanquisher of imperialism and so on, according to your perception, and one man's perception was rather strange. 'Long live the unifier of religions!' he was heard to shout, and a bewildered listener pricked up his ears and wanted to make sure of the slogan. 'Why the unifier of religions? The Muslims are still Muslims, the Jews are still Jews and the Christians are still Christians.' 'Are they?' said the demonstrator. 'Hasn't he made them all give up believing in God?' (*talla'hum min dinhum*).

As expected, the bulk of jokes smack of middle-class concerns, like the one about a fellow who went to the Sudan and amassed great wealth, with which he proudly returned to Egypt. As soon as he arrived, the demands for payment of taxes, social security contributions, stamp duties and so on started to pour in until he was reduced to the pauper he had been before his emigration to the Sudan, living simply on bread and helva. 'Wait a minute,' said he to the grocer, 'can you, in Allah's name, wrap the helva in another newspaper?'

'What difference does it make?' asked the grocer.

'This one has a picture of Jamal Abd al-Nasser. He'll be sure to lick off my helva.'

The explosion of political humour in Nasser's time should be a classic example for the thesis that laughter emanates from the discrepancy between reality and conception and the sudden collapse of expectation, at least in so far as the middle class was concerned. Nasser's great promises were destined to founder on the hard and sad realities of Egypt's past and present, and the observer's expectation received the jolt of a magnificent rider coming to a halt in a quagmire. A poor woman was repeatedly irritated by her husband's preoccupation with politics and enthusiasm for Nasser and his Socialist Union Party. 'Look at you! What have you gained out of Nasser and all your talk about his party. Why don't you go and ask him? What have we gained out of him?' The woman defied her husband and the wretched man decided to take up her challenge and go and see the leader. After listening to his story, Nasser asked him to go to the window and tell him what he saw. There were the beautiful presidential gardens, the well-kept streets around, the lofty palaces and four-star hotels of Cairo. 'Now go to your wife and tell her,' said Nasser, 'in ten years more under the Socialist Union, the whole of Egypt will be like this.'

The man was very impressed and hurried home to tell his wife. 'Go to the window and tell me what you see.' The wife went to the window of their hovel and started to count. There was the open cesspit stinking in the heat, the children, in rags, fighting over a mouldy biscuit, the rubbish heap , the rusty dumped cars, etc., etc. 'Ten years more under the Socialist Union and the whole of Egypt will be like this,' said her husband.

This is a striking example of Herbert Spencer's 'descending incongruity' igniting the mechanism of laughter – from the sublime to the ridiculous, from the imaginary to the actual. Nasser's social gains were not designed for the fat middle class and feudalist slobs, but rather made at their expense, and the fairer distribution of the same small cake meant less cake for them.

'How is life treating you these days?' said one journalist to another.

'Oh, fine, thanks be to Allah. Three days a week Um Kulthum's songs, two days football and one day meat,' said the other.

Of course, part of the problem was the bureaucratic organization of the state-run economy, especially the ill-managed retail shops and co-operatives, which were often short of the items most needed. Instead of looking into the cause of the shortages, an inspector advised the store manager to re-educate the public and advise them on using substitutes for the missing goods. He could offer them cabbage instead of lettuce, soap instead of toothpaste, and so on. As it happened, a customer called and asked for toilet paper, which was not available, but the manager remembered his inspector's advice and said, 'Sorry, we ran out of that, but we have something as good or even better.' He went inside and came back with a pack of sand paper.

Against that, Nasser made considerable concessions to the poorer classes, including health insurance, unemployment benefits and family allowances. A man was seen leading his pregnant wife, in labour, to hospital, forging his way in the midst of the congested pavements and shouting at the crowds, 'Mind the allowance! Mind the allowance!' This is just the kind of thing an Egyptian would say, for I myself heard a pedlar at Khan al-Khalili selling some rather horrid, cheap-looking knickers with these words: 'Pants for your mother-in-law! Gifts for your mother-in-law!'

In fact, one can have a great deal of fun in Cairo by simply listening carefully to the sardonic, tongue-in-the-cheek way in which ordinary people give the most mundane things of life political dimensions. The late president wanted, of course, to surround his regime with a halo of secrecy and efficient intelligence whose success was described by Mustafa Amin by saying that his apparatus knew everything about every girlfriend of General Moshe Dayan but nothing about the troops and tanks which he mobilized for the attack on Sinai. Among Nasser's secret enterprises were the air-force aerodromes in the desert. But if you had travelled along the Cairo–Alexandria desert road by bus, you would have most certainly heard the bus conductor calling at the top of his voice as the vehicle reached the bus stop of that location: 'The secret aerodromes!'

This may be part of history, but the next anecdote is part of the fiction which is truer than life. A detective was briefed by his boss to contact another detective at a certain café, with such and such name and descriptions. The man went to the café and asked its owner to direct him to the right person.

'Yes, but what Hussein?' said the café owner. 'We've many Husseins here. There is Hussein the porter, Hussein the carpenter, Hussein the plumber . . . which Hussein do you want?'

The detective then gave him the description he had.

'Oh, you want Hussein the spy,' said the owner, 'Why didn't you say so?'

And as loud and clear as he could, he shouted to the customers: 'Hussein the spy! Hussein the spy! There is a visitor here for you.'

It is said that Hamlet was Shakespeare's greatest failure. If we are to borrow and adapt this epigram, we may well say that Nasser was the Arabs' greatest political failure. He did so much good for the cause of his country and his Arab nation and – alas – so much wrong. In considering all the facets of his rule and all that has been said about him in jest and in earnest, one cannot help recalling Bergson's words; 'We laugh not only at the faults of our fellow men, but also, at times, at their good qualities.'

'Which Way to Go?' George Bahjuri 1985. (The word in the speech bubble is 'agreement?'; all the arrows on the signpost say 'disagreement'.)

7 The Trauma of the Naksa

> We laughed and our laughter was a folly.
> It is right that the people of this earth should cry.
>
> Al-Ma'arri

The 1967 war with Israel was unquestionably the most traumatic experience suffered by the Arab World, reaching its climax of anguish with the resignation of President Nasser. As we heard it over the radio, a young Egyptian woman could not stand it any longer and buried her face in a sofa and started sobbing, while a friend known for his strength and cheerful spirit rushed to the lavatory and reappeared minutes later with bloodshot eyes. Two days later, we met in the common room of the School of Oriental and African Studies in London, where I related the odd story of an Indonesian Muslim brother who rang the Iraqi Embassy to volunteer for the war. 'You didn't do well in this war', he told me. 'I should like to come and help you fight the Israelis. I am very good at judo.' As I reached the word 'judo' I burst into uncontrollable laughter, which infected my listeners instantly and the whole débâcle of the set-back, or what the Arabs decided to call *naksa*, suddenly became a piece of black comedy on an epic scale, as our jokes flowed on and on. Did you hear of the broom-and-basket maker of Amman who stuck a notice outside his shop saying 'Military Zone. Photography Prohibited'. Why did he do that. Well, he heard King Hussein exhorting the people to fight Israel even with their brooms.

The way the Egyptian officers ran away from Sinai to the safety of Cairo became a world-wide scandal and Egypt's wits could not resist contributing their own. A young lieutenant in a hurry ran after one of Cairo's crowded buses and just managed to get in when he was flung into the lap of an old woman who held him by the shoulder and said tenderly: 'Hi sonny, still running?'

The Arabs wondered what would happen to the lost territories and whether they would ever recover them. Egypt's Commander-in-

Chief, Field Marshal Amin, was horrified to see President Nasser ordering a tattoo artist to print on his right arm the names of all the territories seized by Israel like Sinai, Gaza, Sharm al-Shaykh, Jerusalem, the Golan Heights.

'Why are you doing this?'

'Lest I should forget them.'

'But why tattooed? What will you do if we get them back?'

'If we get them back I'll cut off my right arm(*Aqta'idi*).'

The June fiasco brought to the surface all the weaknesses of the 'revolutionary' military regimes, and their critics pounced on the opportunity to bring to ridicule all their failures. In Egypt, the most vociferous voice of this new spirit evolved from the partnership of Ahmad Fu'ad Najm, the vernacular poet, and Shaykh Imam, the blind lutanist with the melancholic voice. Between them, they took up old melodies and adapted them to the most bitter verses which the shaykh sang to the accompaniment of his lute in cafés, private homes and, when possible, public concerts. Their fame spread throughout the Arab World as they voiced the despair of the general masses with such songs as 'Oh, how lovely, the return of our officers from the front line!':

> Praise be to Allah, we hugged ourselves in joy
> Oh, how lovely the return of our officers from the front line!
> O, people of Egypt which is defended by thieves
> Plenty of beans, falafil and buildings
> Don't talk of Sinai and the rest and so on
> Three hundred buses are still running packed
> What is one million dead, or the whole world?
> Life is not guaranteed and every soul has its fate.
> The people are in bleak humiliation, so what?
> Utterly lost! Just don't tell us 'We are revolutionaries.'
> Whether at Aqaba we ran away or in Sinai,
> Defeat will teach us to forget our freedom,
> Praise be to Allah, we hugged ourselves in joy
> Oh, how lovely, the return of our officers from the front line!

This is a very bitter song, but not as bitter as the next one, racy and caustic both in its rhythm and its diction:

> Shurum burum with such heedless people!

And such heedlessness which blocked their senses.
The dog went barking in the party.
While most of the listeners were dead drunk.
Allah, Allah, my country, the land of trinkets.
Our condition pleases no man
The beggar will not put up with our lot
But, oh, what a tongue we have
If we applied it to steel, it would melt it.
Allah, Allah, my country, the land of trinkets.

Najm had never attacked Nasser directly, but as soon as Sadat
took over, he lost no time in attacking the President of the country,
'the wide-mouthed revolutionary gipsy':

> Some days he is a Marxist
> Some days he is a pacifist
> A friend of all rulers
> And sixteen other nations
> Oh, how sweet to see him
> Brooding over the destiny of mankind!

In Syria, another partnership was formed by Muhammad al-
Maghut and Durayd Lahham, who gave vent to similar thoughts but
in dramatic form, as in their most famous musicals, *Dhay'at Tishrin*
(The October Village) and *Kasak ya Watan* (Cheerio, My Country!).
In *The October Village*, we sense the tension of the country as the
nightwatchman orders the young bride to shut the window. It is
curfew time and thoughts and looks are not allowed to wander
about. Therefore, her lover is forced to come to her window in a
dustbin. Just before her wedding, thieves come and occupy her
dowry, a vineyard, and all considerations of love and marriage are
immediately shelved, pending the recovery of the vineyard. It is an
obvious parody about the loss of the Golan Heights to the Israelis. In
the attempt to persuade the *mukhtar* (village head) to do something,
the whole edifice of the corrupt and idiotic world of officialdom is
exposed.

The *mukhtar* discovers an idea to retrieve the vineyard but, alas,
thieves come and steal it from him. 'How often have I told you to
lock the windows when you think?' says the watchman.

'Bring the police dog!' says Ghawwar. 'Let it smell the head of the
mukhtar and release it to sniff about for his idea.'

The *mukhtar* eventually strikes upon a plan, i.e. to create

divisions and feuds among the villagers and thus make them forget
the vineyard. He instructs the watchman to kill the cow and leave
Ghawwar's name by its side. 'But what has the cow done to kill it?'
asks the watchman.

'Is it necessary for any one to commit something before killing
him?' says the *mukhtar*.

The plan succeeds and the village is plunged into strife. 'Turn the
radio on London. Let us know what is going on here,' shouts
someone.

The *mukhtar* is finally toppled and another takes his place, then a
third one and a fourth, but in reality they are all the same man, only
with different masks. Each time, the new *mukhtar* delivers a hair-
raising speech of a kind familiar now to Arab ears, and in every case
the villagers are warned against the new plot just discovered.

'In all parts of the world,' says Naif, 'they discover oil and iron ore,
except in this village. They discover only plots.'

Naif is then arrested for complaining that there was a shortage of
foodstuffs. The village ran out of milk because the nationalized cow
had ten bureaucrats appointed to attend to its milking and the shy
cow froze. Naif was tortured. 'Why do you spread such rumours?
Look at the *mukhtar*'s house! It's packed with provisions – rice,
whisky, meat, *burghal*. Everything is there.' Naif is then followed to
the torture chamber by Ghawwar who assures them that he said
nothing.

'Here is the danger. Here is plotting more serious than Naif's. Naif
spoke and we know what is in his mind. But you said nothing and we
don't know what you are up to.'

'You mean we aren't safe when we speak, and we aren't safe when
we shut up?'

'What are you?'

'I am nothing. I am the citizen. Nothing at all.'

He is then asked to sign his admission.

'Sign for what?'

'The things which you would have liked to say.'

A new *mukhtar* decides to attack the thieves and Ghawwar,
limping from the effect of torture, leads the army, while the boss
gives, from his balcony, a running communiqué on the attack. 'Our
men have killed ten of the thieves,' says he behind his binoculars.

'But the thieves are only three,' says the bride.

'Of course, binoculars enlarge things, don't they?'

The fighters retreat without a fight and the *mukhtar* proceeds to
defend his failure to lead them and the importance of his staying

alive. 'Have you ever heard of a village without a *mukhtar*?'

A young man answers back, 'Have you ever heard of a *mukhtar* without a village?'

Ghawwar the clown and dissipated drunkard confronts the *mukhtar*: 'What homeland is this?... They took me to prison with my shoes size 41, and I came out with size 45 ... You want us to defend the prisons which have become more numerous than our schools ... With none of us daring to open his mouth except when in the dentist's chair ...

One, of course, wonders how the play was allowed a performance in its home, but the writers did the old trick of giving their play a flattering ending. As the *mukthar* is chastised and reminded of his promises and high ideals, he reforms and dedicates himself to the task of liberating the vineyard, which he achieves with a rousing, patriotic song. The audiences clapped with great enthusiasm and missed the cynical joke – or did they? As it happened, the Syrian authorities went on performing the play, assuming that it applied to Iraq and the Iraqis went on performing it assuming that it applied to Syria!

A few years later, Durayd Lahham, the comedian and co-author, justified the unavoidable spirit of compromise with this lame explanation: 'The writer and artist must have a self-censorship – in the sense that he may have many things to say ... because the circumstances of the country are more important than his freedom of thought.'[1]

Cheerio, My Country is a series of sketches in which the same comic figure, Ghawwar, projects the frustrations of his people. His one-year-old daughter dies in his arms as he is kept waiting for the doctor who is preoccupied with treating a top bureaucrat suffering from sexual impotence, and the crying father receives some kind words: 'The little girl will be in paradise.'

'She couldn't find a place in the ambulance. She couldn't find a place in the hospital. How do you think she will find a place in paradise?' says Ghawwar.

Well, this is all the result of imperialism, he is told as they take him to prison for his habitual grumbling. There they bring his file and show him how they knew everything he had said or done.

'You knew all those things about me and yet you didn't know that my children had nothing to eat yesterday.'

Ghawwar is unable to maintain his children and decides to sell them. Why not? People are selling their country nowadays. Why not sell their children? Persuading a woman with a dog to buy one of them, he assures her that her dog would love to have his son for a plaything. To another purchaser, he recommends his third son as one who swallows up anything in his way. Oh, no, says the man. Oh, yes, says Ghawwar. Just wait for him until he is old enough to work at the Ministry of Economy. He will swallow up all its assets.

In another sketch, a radio discussion programme is presented with such interlocution:

'The latest news is that Israel has attacked the south of Lebanon.'

'And where are the Arabs?'

'They have just launched their own attacks.'

'On whom?'

'On each other.'

Hampered by their incorrigible intransigence, the Arabs could make no headway with their attempt to recover the occupied territories by diplomacy, and Nasser's war of attrition simply backfired. The impasse was complete and the death of the Arab leader seems now to have been the only means to break into a new direction. When Sadat took over, he was rated as a man with little skill and no intelligence, and his furtive ways and secrecy in preparing for his strike against Israel left his countrymen cold and sceptical of his abilities to do anything. One evening, he was late for a concert which he wanted to attend. So were Um Kalthum and Najua Fu'ad. The three decided to slip in quietly from a back door, where a policeman stopped them and asked them to prove what they claimed to be. Um Kalthum raised her voice with one refrain and the policeman immediately recognized in her the great singer. Najua Fu'ad wiggled her hips and the officer saw that she was the same famous dancer. 'What about you? Do something to prove that you are Anwar al-Sadat,' he said to the president.

'I don't know – I can't do anything.'

The officer then beckoned him in, 'Oh, then you must be Anwar al-Sadat.'

In another anecdote, he was portrayed as dim and a proper ass. The economic plight hit everybody including the donkeys of al-Manufia, Sadat's village, who met and discussed their problem. 'But we have our brother as head of this country. Let us go to him.' The donkeys organized a delegation, which was kindly received by the president, and their spokesman put their problem most eloquently to him. Upon their return to the village, the rest of the donkeys asked them what the president had said about the problem. 'He is still trying to understand it', the delegates replied. Success, however, made him indulge more copiously in the native habit of patronizing and he went on to call everybody 'my son' regardless of any obvious discordance. It is said that after the Muslim-Coptic clashes, he sacked Shnuda, the Coptic Pope, called him to his office and gave him a long lecture on the importance of religious harmony and tolerance.

'Father Shnuda, listen to me, my son. I don't want any more discrimination between Christians and Muslims. As one responsible for it all, you, my son, will be removed and a new Pope appointed in your place.'

'And who will be the new Pope?'

'Muhammad Ramadan.'

'But Muhammad Ramadan is a Muslim.'

'Good God! Are we back again?'

Although the new president lost no opportunity to bless the soul of the late President Nasser and reaffirm the continuation of his policies, in reality he did nothing but reverse those policies internally and externally. One day he came to a T-junction and his chauffeur asked him which way to turn.

'Which way would our lost leader, President Nasser, have turned?' he asked the chauffeur.

'To the left, Your Excellency.'

'All right then,' said Sadat, 'indicate left and turn right.'

The man who did not know what to do finally dumbfounded the world with his dramatic visit to Jerusalem and the eventual peace accord with Israel, but although the deal was generally endorsed by the Egyptians, his critics went on to lash out at him even more ferociously. The traditional resort to smut and sexual slandering was topped up with the charge of drug addiction. An aggrieved captain in the army sought an interview with him to put his case and was nervous about the meeting. Friends advised him to build up his courage with some whisky and the officer drank until he began to see not only double but treble. He was admitted to see the president who was all by himself, sitting and smoking his marijuana.

'Your Excellency, if you don't mind sending away the two men sitting with you. My case is rather personal.'

'Well then, if it is personal, why are you bringing with you five other captains?'

Upon his death, he was met in the second world by Field Marshal Amir, another victim of the same charge. 'Oh, golly, show us how much hashish you have brought us from earth.'

'Are you crazy?' replied Sadat. 'Bring hash with me when my whole funeral was packed with nobody other than plainclothes policemen!'

His open-door policies did not achieve the desired results and the satirists found ample food for their jibes, especially in reference to Israel. News reports had it that Sadat was about to strike a deal to sell the Nile water for the irrigation of the Negev.

'Have you heard? They are going to ration soap.'

'What has soap got to do with the sale of the Nile water?'

'Well, you need water to use soap, don't you?'

It must be interesting to compare the jokes made about Nasser and those about his successor. As can be deduced from Chapter 6, Nasser's jokes were usually about his regime, his socialism, his suppression, but hardly ever about his person; they hovered around him but never dared to touch him; they were almost said in love, a kind of friendly teasing and political titillation. Sadat's jokes were caustic, vicious and almost always personal and scandalous. 'Of course, Nasser was stupid,' someone said. 'How else can you explain his appointment of an ass for a successor?' After the restoration of Sinai to Egypt, a delegation from al-Arish visited President Sadat to thank him for all his efforts. When asked what they wanted to see of Cairo, they said that there was only one place which they wanted to visit and pray at – Nasser's tomb. Anwar al-Sadat, however, was not short of ammunition and gave as much as he received. His acting ability not only helped him in charming the Americans but also in ridiculing his foes in the Arab World with his glib tongue and teasing innuendoes. His friends, including the writer, Yusif Idris, found him witty and full of humour.

One of the most important consequences of the *naksa* was the emergence of the Palestinian guerrilla movement under the leadership of Yasser Arafat. The charismatic Arafat proved to be more resourceful in diplomacy than in warfare and his long survival on the eternal tightrope which he walks does credit to any politician. This has distanced him from the prevailing verbal slanging matches and deprived him of the fun and humour associated with them, but then very few guerrilla fighters have any sense of humour, for laughter is a deflation of energy and violence is an explosion of it. Relying almost exclusively on the goodwill and approbation of his suppliers and supporters, he mastered the technique of keeping in with everybody. During an Umra pilgrimage to Mecca, he was given the traditional seven stones to cast on the devil at Muna. His guide noticed that he had cast only six and slipped the seventh one in his pocket.

'Abu Ammar, you have thrown only six stones on the devil!' said the guide.

'Yes, I thought I shouldn't really cut all lines with him.'

It is quite a benign joke showing some measure of the respect which is felt for the Palestinian leader.

Ignored by the world, let down by their Arab leaders, and chased mercilessly by the Israelis, his Palestinian people seem, for all intents and purposes, doomed to an eternal life in refugee camps. The only hope was in the Kingdom of God, until they received this report. God sat on his throne to distribute the nations each to its place until the turn of the Palestinians came.

'To hell with them,' said God.

'Sorry,' said Lucifer, 'it is completely full up in hell.'

'Well then, let them go to paradise,' said God.

'Sorry,' said St Peter, 'it's chock-a-block in paradise.'

God thought and then said, 'All right, put them in tents!'

Naksa is an apt description of the 1967 débâcle and its aftermath, for it means reversion to a worse state. Ever since that fateful 5 June, things have been deteriorating for the Arab World all the time and many Arab commentators raised their arms in despair and concluded that things could never be worse. Arab commentators, however, always reach the wrong conclusions, for every time they had said so, things did become worse. The downhill slide drifted to the bloody fratricide of Lebanon, where a Christian priest and a Muslim shaykh sat for hours on end waiting to see the prime minister amid the noise of rockets and machine guns. The priest finally opened his mouth in despair: 'There is no God except Allah and Muhammad is Allah's messenger.'

The shaykh pricked up his ears: 'What is this, Father? You have pronounced the Islamic *shahada* [attestation of Islamic faith]!'

'Such goings on make anyone blaspheme,' said the priest.

The fratricide took the macabre form of killing passers-by point-blank on merely suspecting them of belonging to the other sect. Thus, a Muslim was stopped at a Christian checkpoint and wanted to save his life by giving himself a false Christian name.

'No, you are not called George and you are not a Christian,' his captors said as they pointed their guns at him.

'I am, I am. I swear by Allah and Muhammad!'

There is no record whether the gunners were tickled into a better sense of Christianity. The leaders held a series of reconciliation conferences with little result. In one bout of talks a militia leader was irritated by the repeated interventions of Taqi al-Din al-Sulh and shouted at him in defiance: 'What business have you to speak here. We represent those who are fighting [*al-Muqatilin*]. Whom do you represent?'

Al-Sulh replied: 'I represent those who have been killed [*al-Maqtulin*].'

Although some eighteen years have passed since the date of that fateful *naksa* of 1967, the Arabs are still in the throes of that trauma without ever finding a way out of its quagmire. With them locked in this unhappy grip, this chapter is bound to remain unfinished, as more comic wits will go on seeking their escape in jokes and jibes.

'The Western media as seen by the Arab World', *Al-Sharq al-Awsat* 1982.

8 The Rifle and the Pen

> If your father is a soldier you may well wiggle with your belly.
>
> Arabic Proverb

When the politicians and ministers of the newly formed state of Iraq gathered at the house of Yusif al-Suwaidi, the prominent leader of the struggle for independence, to plan the budget allocations, the item for the Ministry of Defence came up for discussion.

'What is this?' said the old man, and his sons explained to him that this was for the army.

'What is the army for?' he went on asking almost incredulously.

An independent state must have a flag and an army, he was told, and the army is necessary for defending the flag from the enemies of the country.

'Why do you assume we'll have enemies? Besides, there is Britain which has more stakes to defend here than any of us.'

The argument was laughed out of court and the old man could only mutter, 'All right, have your way, but mark my words – you will be sorry for it.'

In less than one decade that army staged the first military coup d'état in the Arab World, in 1936, and the country was dominated until 1941 by the Golden Square, a group of four colonels who dismissed cabinets and formed new ones at will. In 1958, the army returned to the political arena to topple the monarchy and set the country on the path of military interventions. In 1952, Egypt's Free Officers removed King Farouk and set up the republic. In Syria, the pattern was repeated with more frequency and the example was emulated in the Yemen, Libya, Algeria, the Sudan and Mauritania. With few exceptions, army officers took charge everywhere in the Arab World, distributing among themselves, their kinsmen and their friends all the coveted positions, ranks, decorations and wealth. At one stage, somebody counted with his fingers and found

that there were five field-marshals in the world; four of them were
Arab. In 1984, the Palestine poet, the late Mu'in Basisu, wrote and
recited in Friends' House in London:

> An epoch that is a wonder,
> Under a copper given the choice Arab names
> With a chameleon on his whip
> Sucking the colour of my blood.
> Bless the prison cell that has become our homeland!
> Bless its name 'wonder'!
> And no wonder
> For a copper hopped on our shoulders,
> And a copper mounted on his shoulders.
> And a copper rebelled against his sergeant,
> The sergeant turned on his general.
> A eunuch pounced on a eunuch
> And from his deformity procured a wonder.
> And no wonder!

Like so much that has happened in the Arab World, the rise of
military regimes can be traced to the 1948 failure in Palestine, which
prompted many army officers, with Nasser in the fore, to conclude
that nothing could be done until the old-style governments were
swept away with all their corruption and inefficiency and replaced
by new revolutionary regimes based on the army. It was a simplistic
conclusion expected from frustrated soldiers and acted upon by
ambitious officers in many parts of the world. The military juntas
cured some afflictions like feudalism, and created new ones, like
totalitarianism, but in general the old complex problems so deeply
rooted in the soil continued as before, if not actually aggravated by
the heavy hand of militarism. The Free Officers did not simply take
over the helm of office but acted like a tribe descending on a city
distributing the spoils among the victors, their kinsmen and their
friends. Officers took over most of the coveted positions in
practically every department. It was reported that General Qasim
invited a university lecturer to join the government:

'I don't mind, if you give me the command of the Fifth Mechanized
Division.'

'But you are not a military officer.'

'What of that? You have appointed a military officer as head of our
Ministry of Education!'

The individualist Arabs have a natural antipathy against the military fortified by the fact that for centuries the soldiery were foreign mercenaries or occupiers. There is a considerable wealth of sayings, nursery rhymes and folklore satirizing the soldier or warning against him. 'No one dares tell a soldier "cover up your chin",' says one proverb. Desertion and evasion of call-up are widespread throughout the Middle East and the Iraqi government had to launch a bloody campaign in the thirties to force tribesmen to accept conscription. A doctor was frustrated by a pregnant mother whose overdue baby resisted all attempts to induce it. Glued to his stethoscope and listening to the foetus, the doctor managed eventually to hear this whimper: 'Have they announced the call-up for the 1982 births?' Of course, the authorities mobilized all the information media to correct this image and present the nationalist armies as liberators as well as defenders, but the wits had a different version to give. A man in a bus stood on the foot of another until the latter could endure it no longer, and opened his mouth.

'Excuse me – are you an officer in the army?'

'No.'

'Is your father an officer in the army?'

'No.'

'Are you married to the daughter of an officer?'

'No.'

'Do you have any relative serving as an officer in the army?'

'No.'

The man then punched him in the face.

'Then how dare you stand on my foot all this time?'

One may laugh at such an anecdote, but it is on record that the Egyptian journalist, Musa Sabri, was suspended from work for criticizing the hairstyle of a television announcer who happened to be the wife of an officer. Of course, the influential minority known as the 'educated class', which did so much to get rid of the foreigners, did not like seeing the captured positions taken over by the men of arms and went on to portray the new rivals as a retarded lot, lacking both education and civilization. The Libyan government, so they related, wanted to despatch its Chief-of-Staff, General Abu Bakr Yunis, to Moscow for negotiations, but the general had always created diplomatic problems by his narrow observance of the Islamic dietary rules, refusing to eat anything suspected to be *haram*. 'For God's sake, don't make things difficult for your hosts. Just eat whatever they give you.' On his arrival in Moscow, the general was presented with a bouquet of flowers – which he gratefully devoured. In another story, he was trying to stand on a shining mahogany table to replace an electric light bulb, when Colonel Gadaffi took note of the precious table and told him to spread a newspaper on it first. 'No, I don't think I'll need the paper. I am tall enough,' said the general.

An Arab minister attending the funeral of a Soviet leader was somewhat bewildered when he saw the mourners drinking vodka after the burial of the dead man and asked his officer ambassador about it. 'It is their custom to drink to his health,' the ambassador answered.

In the wake of the Bandung Conference, the Indian Prime Minister, Mr Nehru, asked Abd al-Hakim Amir to urge President Nasser on certain delicate issues regarding non-alignment, and the field-marshal promised to do so. Just before boarding the aeroplane, the anxious Nehru repeated his request and begged Amir to keep it in mind. 'Of course, of course! What do you think I am? An Indian?' The popularity and absolute naturalism of the anecdote prompted other Arab nations to adapt it to their various military leaders.

The wits are still considering the profile of President Husni Mubarak, former air-force pilot, but tentative sketches seem to cast him in the same mould of daft soldier. Recognizing his limitations in public speaking, he asked his secretary to prepare for him a five-minute speech, which he went on rehearsing and punctuating until he called for his secretary again. 'I asked you for a five-minute speech. This one is taking twenty minutes.'

'Your Excellency,' said the secretary, 'these are four copies.'

When only Egypt was ruled by a military junta, things were not too bad, but when almost every Middle-Eastern country had its own military junta, the situation became quite chaotic and the trail of chaos rumbled on from the day General Qasim eliminated the royalist regime of Iraq. Soon after his accession to office, he struck up a close friendship with Mr Nichkin, the First Secretary of the Soviet Embassy in Baghdad. During one of their long *tête-à-tête* sessions at the Ministry of Defence, the call for prayer was heard from the minaret and Mr Nichkin rose from his chair to break up the conversation in due respect to the call. General Qasim was amused and expressed his astonishment at the sight of the atheist representative of the Marxist state observing such duty to God. 'I have been an atheist all my life,' said the Soviet envoy, 'but ever since I came to this country I have recognized that there must be a God, otherwise how else can we explain anything functioning here at all?'

Qasim's military regime clashed with Nasser's military regime and its Ba'athist supporters, and in that clash, Arab political satire reached its zenith in modern times with chilling implications. Among the stories circulated at the time was the case of the thief who was chased by the police in the Shurja Bazzar. To the mobs running after him with ropes to grab him and drag him, he was heard shouting. 'A thief! A thief! I swear by Allah I am only a thief – not a Ba'athist.' The most vulgar caricatures, lampoons and rhymes covered the walls of the schools, colleges, cafés, cinemas and shops of Baghdad, but nothing in this genre of sinister humour could have matched what went on in the 'People's Court' of Colonel Mahdawi, often called by Qasim's opponents the 'circus'. Mahdawi, the President of the Court, was somewhat interested in literature and wrote some poetry, none of which was published, and the People's Court gave him the one chance of his life to exhibit his wares and indulge in sadistic humour at the expense of the accused. He had the habit of interrupting them, often for the purpose of reciting some verses, but one man outdid him in this method and kept on interrupting the President of the Court himself until he was forced to shout at the accused: 'Excuse me, am I not entitled to freedom of expression?' I was often tempted to compare the antics of his court with that of Asdak in Brecht's *Caucasian Chalk Circle.*

Ever since that People's Court, military tribunals, meting out hard justice and easy injustice, were set up in most Arab countries and it has become the fashion for soldiers to try prisoners of conscience with their complex thoughts and ideologies, producing some fine pieces of black comedy. In a one-act play written by Yusif al-Ani, *Ras al-Shilila,* the presiding military judge sentences a rather large group of detainees by this method: 'All those standing to the left of the man in the yashmak, three years with hard labour. All those to the right of the man in the yashmak, seven years with hard labour.'

Many of these military judges must have found their judicial roles bewildering and confusing. A lawyer used his friendship with a judge to influence him in favour of his client and the judge promised everything, but he got it all mixed up and sentenced the man to ten years.

'What have you done? You have given my client ten years!' said the advocate to the judge later.

'Oh, I am sorry. I promise, I'll owe you ten years. Next time you have a client, remind me of it and I'll take it off him.'

Of course, people don't tell such anecdotes as jokes but as gospel truth, which in many instances is quite the case, as in Mahdawi's People's Court.

Everyone is free to his own interpretation and speculation but the following piece is a verbatim extract from an official decree issued to give amnesty to army deserters[1]:

> a) Those who committed the crimes of desertion or absence and who have failed to rejoin their units during the validity period of this decision shall be punished by execution. Those who committed the crime of absence for a period of more than five days without any legitimate reason, or the crime of desertion, shall receive the same punishment. b) The punishment shall be doubled in the case of those who commit the crimes of default or violation by failing to rejoin their units within the set period.

Many are the jokes coined about military justice like the one about the man seen scurrying home anxiously.

'Why are you in such a haste, Ahmad?'

'Haven't you heard? They have decided to cut the penis of any man with three testicles.'

'But you haven't three testicles, have you?'

'No, I haven't. But here they cut first and count later.'

The old story about the jackal had a new lease of life under Nasser. A wolf saw the jackal running in great haste towards the border of the Sudan.

'Why are you running so, my dear friend?'

'They are short of meat and have decided to kill all buffaloes.'

'But you are not a buffalo.'

'No, but by the time I convince the soldiers that I am not a buffalo my skin would have reached the tannery.'

There is no doubt that under a military dictatorship, one may easily perish without the good sense of the jackal, as happened to a poor fellow who treated the curfew order too lightly and got himself killed. 'Why have you shot this man? It is not curfew time yet,' said the officer to his sergeant.

'I know this man,' replied the sergeant. 'He lives on the other side of the town and he wouldn't have made it to his house before curfew time.'

As it happened, the comic element in Qasim's regime and his Mahdawi's Court could not escape the notice of the Hadramauti playwright, Ali Ahmad Baktir, who satirized the entire regime in his play *The Sole Leader.* The lieutenants of the Sole Leader (General Qasim) become apprehensive about his safety and decide to find a double to impersonate him, but their search can produce none so identical with the leader other than the shoeshine, Qazman. The disgusted leader rebels against this fact but they assure him that the similarity is very compelling. 'Just like the similarity of a pair of shoes.' They start teaching the shoeshine all the manners and mannerisms of the revolutionary government and rabble-rousing oratory, and training, at the same time, the Sole Leader in the art of polishing any shoes put before him, whether coming from the east, the west or any other direction. The new shoeshine, however, insists on his lieutenants addressing him with his full titles before polishing their shoes and al-Yawar (otherwise Colonel Wasfi Tahir) starts thus: 'O, our Sole Leader, Saviour of all Arabs, our awaited Messiah, our unique genius, the maker of Arab history, the invincible giant, the great hero, father of politics, the far-sighted oracle, the most important figure in the universe, the leader whose light eclipses all other suns and stars, O vanquisher of imperialism, I beg you to clean my shoes as you have cleaned the Arab nation from the dust of reaction and humiliation.'

Both the leader and his double excel in their new jobs – Qazman running amok at his state functions and receptions and the Sole Leader polishing shoes with extreme humbleness – so much so that their nearest and dearest can hardly tell who is who. Lest such confusion should affect his own wife, the Sole Leader informs her of a certain bite on the right ear. The play, richer in political indictment than in sparkling wit, concludes with the inevitable next coup and the Sole Leader is arrested and hanged outside the Ministry of Defence. But was he the real Sole Leader or was he Qazman the shoeshine? Only the wife could tell and the wife finds that bite mark on his right ear. Baktir, however, decides to leave the fortunes of such military leaders in menacing ambiguity as he indicates in his play that the Sole Leader made a mistake in placing that bite mark. The poet al-Qirdawi (the Monkey[2]) ends the play with these words: 'Haven't I said, gentlemen, the entire reality has become a joke?'

Conversely, the joke also became a reality and Baktir's play was enacted in earnest in February 1963 as other units of the Iraqi Army under the direction of the underground Ba'ath Party moved on Baghdad and executed the Sole Leader at the Ministry of Defence. The operation ushered in a new era of a series of military coups in both Iraq and Syria, engineered by the various factions of the party which advocated the adoption of the 'coup' as the means of historical change and based its strength mainly on army officers hailing from the poor rural provinces where the bourgeois values of freedom, democracy and human rights were not top priorities. The tough

Ba'athists inaugurated their rule by settling accounts with the communists, their erstwhile tormentors, and the communists launched a world-wide campaign against the Ba'ath. In Russia, Iraqi comrades called on the Imam of the Leningrad Mosque to denounce the Ba'athists in his Friday sermon. Having listened to their long accounts of woes and atrocities, the good old Imam from Uzbekistan gasped in horror, 'By Allah, these Ba'athists must be worse that the communists.'

The story was related to the President of Iraq and, I am told, he roared with laughter. Coercive discipline was imposed to force uniform obedience to the state and the party. A man was quizzed upon his death by the two angels of reckoning, Munkar and Nakir.

'What is your religion?'

'The Ba'ath.'

'Who is your God?'

'Michel Aflaq.'

'Who is your Prophet?'

'President Bakr.'

The puzzled angels, who had never heard of such a religion before, took the man with them and went up to God to report his strange case, and God decided to ask him: 'What is your religion?'

'Islam.'

'Who is your God?'

'Allah.'

'Who is your Prophet?'

'Muhammad.'

Now God himself was puzzled. 'Why didn't you say so straight away to the angels of death?'

'I thought they were interrogators from the Security Department.'

Arab humorists played on the name of Asad, the President of Syria whose personality was built up, like elsewhere, into a cult. A tourist was intrigued as he noticed that practically all the main streets and squares of Syrian cities were given the name of Asad. After a quick look in his Arabic dictionary, he found that the word meant 'lion'. Having increased his Arabic vocabulary by one word, he turned to his guide and said: 'Don't you know any other animal to call your streets after?' In another anecdote, which bears a foreign import hallmark, a man found an old painting of Christ Crucified and sold it to an antique dealer for ten thousand liras. A friend heard this story, remembered a painting of President Asad which was thrust upon him, and took it to the same dealer, but was offered only a few liras for it.

'How is that? You have paid ten thousand liras for Christ Crucified and offer me only a few liras for our President Asad?'

'Well, if you bring me Asad crucified, I'll pay you twice ten thousand.'

Another man found a better function for the new, prestigious flyover in Damascus and started to use the ground below as a public convenience. The authorities were infuriated and put a policeman next to a soiled pillar. Seeing the policeman there the following day, the man simply went to another pillar and did the same. A second policeman was posted to that pillar and the man was forced to got to a third one. After a few more days a policeman was put at every pillar. 'My God!' said the man as he came again and saw this concentration of police, 'President Asad must be coming here to piss.'

The authorities accustomed themselves to rewarding party members with Mercedes cars. A Syrian on a visit to West Germany was impressed by what he saw in the multi-storey car parks of Hamburg. 'Our Ba'ath Party branch must be doing well here,' he observed.

One of the saddest events which rocked Syria and indeed the whole world, was the destruction of the old Medina of Hamah, which has a traditional competition with Damascus. A gentleman from that town told another from Damascus: 'You know, our town has entered the annals of history.' 'Yes,' replied the man from Damascus, 'but it has also gone off the map.'

The military, who took over for the declared purpose of combating corruption, succeeded only in developing it, thanks to the suppression of public criticism and press exposure. In a military parade, the spectators were impressed by the way the police dogs turned their eyes towards the presidential pavilion on the whisper of one word from their trainer. 'What did you say to them?' he was asked.

'Oh, just the same word they are trained for: "thieves".'

In another anecdote about Sadat, the late Egyptian president joined President Carter and President Brezhnev in a space flight.

'We must now be over Washington,' said Carter, and his companions asked him how he knew. 'Look! My watch is flashing with a green light from the Pentagon.'

A little while later, Brezhnev said, 'We must now be over Moscow.' In answer to the same query, he said, 'Listen! My watch is playing the "Internationale".'

Minutes later, Sadat said, 'We must now be over Cairo.' And how did you know, they asked. 'Look,' said he as he showed them his wrist with no watch at all, 'Somebody nicked my watch.'

They took whatever they could: double salaries, the prettiest women, highest honours, medals, decorations, ranks, PhD degrees, academic qualifications, and so on. One military leader was annoyed with his son who got ninety-nine per cent in his university examination. 'Why couldn't you get full marks?' said the father.

'Is it my fault that they didn't let me sit for the exam?' said the son.

One of the military rulers who showed a rare sense of humour among his colleagues was President Ja'far al-Numairi of the Sudan, who seemed to enjoy his frank repartee with his friends and enemies. During the 1982 strike he met a delegation from the trade unions to discuss the strikers' grievances and demands for higher wages. Their spokesman dwelt on the economic plight of the workers and the shortages in essential materials: no cooking oil to be found in the market, no sugar, no meat, no potatoes, no nothing. 'For what do you want extra wages then?' asked the president.

This is somehow a reminder of Tawfiq al-Suwaidi's interjection when he was asked to increase the salaries of the civil servants. 'What will they do with more money?' said the Iraqi Prime Minister. 'They will only use it to get more drunk and swear at me.'

In the sad story of the politician who was put in prison, one of Numairi's ministers called on the president to intercede on his behalf. He assured him that he was a very loyal subject and only a week before his arrest 'he was defending you against a whole gang of enemies who were saying foul things about you.'

'And what was he doing sitting with a whole gang of my enemies?' said the president.

However, one cannot help the feeling that Numairi's sudden convertion to Islamic fundamentalism was a further extension of his sense of humour with that big orgy of bottle smashing. But one customs officer was surprised to see one stack of whisky bottles left completely intact. 'Why haven't you smashed this lot?' he asked the porters.

'Don't you see the Numairis' initials on the bottle – J.B.?' (Jafar and Buthaina Numairi).

Numairi's religious brainstorm and its hard strictures depressed the Sudanese middle class which could find no better expression for its frustration than to borrow the joke about Menachem Begin. A Russian, an Englishman, an American and a Sudanese found themselves in hell and wanted to speak to their spouses and hear how things were faring on earth. The Russian took the telephone, dialled the number, inserted ten thousand roubles and got through to his family. The Englishman put in a thousand pounds and got through to his wife; the American put in two thousand dollars and got through; the Sudanese put in three piasters and got through to Khartoum. His mates in hell were surprised – 'Why only three piasters to Khartoum?' they asked him. 'It is a local call,' answered the Sudanese.

The wars fought by the Arabs called for even more recourse to escapist humour, whether in Nasser's adventure in the Yemen, the bloody fratricide of Lebanon or along the Iraqi–Iranian frontiers, where the Kurds volunteered to fight for and against one and all. Nowhere was their position made so unequivocally clear as in the anecdote about one of their fighting sons who shot three Iranian aircraft from his lofty summit. His feat was reported to President Saddam Hussein who hastened to invite him to his palace and honour him like so many devoted patriots who received from his hands the highest medals. The Iraqi President was very impressed by this simple fighter and asked him how he had managed to do what he had done with his ordinary rifle. 'Oh, shooting three Iranian aeroplanes is nothing. Only from the Iraqis I shot down five.'

I tried to find out what kind of jokes the military might have invented against *ashab al-qalam* (the people of the pen), but I could not find any. After all, the military have no need for that. They have the gun.

'Way Out of the Lebanese Crisis', Habib Haddad, *Al-Mustaqbal*
1983

9 The Vernacular Poets

What is known as standard or classical Arabic is basically the language spoken some fourteen centuries ago and kept alive to a large extent all this time because of the compelling effect of the Holy Qur'an. Yet this has not prevented the ordinary people from developing their own everyday language in response to the developments of all those centuries, with the result of a wider gap between the spoken and the written language of Arabic than exists between the two branches in most other languages. The dramatists, novelists and film-script writers and directors face this formidable problem continuously, and the poets receive their inspiration more from the people who lived centuries ago (in the case of the traditionalists), or thousands of miles away (in the case of the modernists) in the West than from the peoples who live around them. The product is something completely alien to the ordinary folk who find their own artistic pleasure in their own vernacular poetry – direct, rich, expressive and throbbing with real life.

From Shakespeare to George Bernard Shaw, writers gave their comic muse the vernacular language and aroused the laughter of millions of spectators by simply injecting the language of the common people into their 'respectable' dialogue. The Arabs are no exception and the Shaykh al-Bishri, much as he was a purist in his written Arabic, could not fail to observe, 'If given in strict Arabic, the joke may lose its lustre and become a dry shell.' In this, al-Bishri was closely following his mentor, Abu Amr al-Jahiz, who wrote as early as the ninth century: 'The ridiculous may be required in certain situations and may become more enjoyable than the joy given by grandiloquent vocabulary and lofty expressions. A very flat (*barida*) joke may also be nicer than a very sharp (*harra*) joke, but the tedium which chills the heart and kills the breath is the lukewarm joke that is neither flat nor sharp. The same applies to middling poetry and middling song. The fun is in the very sharp or the very flat.'[1]

It is significant that when the popular newspapers appeared in Cairo in the nineteenth century, the authorities prohibited them from using the vernacular in dealing with political matters.[2] One wonders whether the authorities made that decision in respect to politics, or in fear of the impact of making political issues more intelligible to the general masses. It may be also significant that these newspapers which published satirical and humorous material in the colloquial suffered more from repression than other newspapers.[3] Such was the case in all Arab countries which witnessed the rise of the vernacular press.

Poetry, of course, takes a central place in the colloquial lore of any nation and the Arabs have more reason to give it such a place. From the very beginning of the satirical press, the *zajal*, the *mawwal*, the *ataba*, the *qasida* and other forms of colloquial poetry have formed an essential section in any humorous publication, and many composers of such poems acquired great fame and popularity among the learned and the illiterate alike. Among these poets stands the unsurpassed Bayram al-Tunisi, whose poetry and political commitment have influenced most Arab vernacular poets. Born in Tunisia and once a labourer in France – before settling in Egypt – Bayram was a revolutionary, an internationalist and a socialist, all after his own fashion, as may be expected from an inspired artist. Unlike other political agitators of his day, he did not see imperialism as the prime cause of all the problems of the Middle East, and concentrated instead on the endemic ills of the socio-political organization of the country. His themes were mainly social, but he also indulged in political matters of an extremely sensitive nature, as in his implied attack on the royal family of Egypt when he ventilated the popular belief, quite serious in the Muslim society of his time, that King Fu'ad married a pregnant lady, and that King Farouk was born four months after the wedding:

> The goose had her neck cut before the celebration.
> The road was opened before the regulation,
> And when the disgraced came for her wedding jubilation
> Silence, said I, do let girls cover up their shame.

'The goose had her neck cut before the celebration' (*al-wazza min gabl al-farah mathbuha*) was on every lip and Bayram was attacked and beaten up repeatedly by the agents of the state, but he was not deterred. In another poem he attacked King Fu'ad directly:

> The English, O Fu'ad, brought and seated you.
> To play on the throne the role of kings

And let you wreak havoc on your father's nation.
Where can they find a fool and a rogue the like of you?

The authorities, tired of him and of beating him up, arrested him and sent him to exile. The wandering life of a refugee took him back to his birthplace in Tunisia, but his own people were no more sympathetic to his ideas than the rest and the same persecution was meted out to him.

> The other, the Muslim Maghribi
> With his silly fez and tassel.
> Shocked, when I criticized him, he said,
> 'Curse upon your father!'
> All I wanted was to see his fetter removed
> But he was happy with it and satisfied.
> Well then, congratulations!

Bayram al-Tunisi attacked almost every social evil, from corruption to bureaucracy and the miscarriage of justice. The following is a little verse on the widespread use of bribery.

> With fifty piasters, you can turn on your loudspeaker
> Well into dawn and longer.
> With fifty piasters, you put a pinch of hash
> Into your enemy's pocket and have him arrested.
> With fifty piasters, you take a certificate
> For your aunt's death, though she still lives.
> With fifty piasters, you rob a pharmacy
> In Cairo's hospitals.
> With fifty piasters, the inspector cancels your fines
> And drops his charges.
> With fifty piasters, you change the charges
> And replace them with ones against me.
> With fifty piasters, your district's mayor
> Let your boys escape the call-up.
> With fifty piasters, you retrieve your wallet,
> With such effect from the pickpocket.
> And with fifty piasters, I write you an article
> Praising you as a man of genius.

Repetition, which is common to all folklore poetry and a pronounced characteristic of Arabic literature, fascinated Bayram al-Tunisi, who used its psychological impact like any experienced propagandist and publicist. In another piece of verbal arabesque, given this time in standard Arabic, he uses his usual whipping boy and symbol of the hated authorities, 'the municipal council', as the key pattern to which all other ideas relate:

> Love has filled me with woes and pain
> Love of the beloved named 'the Municipal Council'.
> Naught has deprived my lovesick eyes of sleep
> Other than the image, the haunting image of the Municipal
>   Council.
> If I earn a loaf, I eat one half,
> And leave the other to the Municipal Council.
> Summer or winter, as I clothe my children,
> I clothe the men of the Municipal Council.
> As if mother, bless her grave, had bequeathed
> And said, 'Your brother is the Municipal Council.'
> I fear to marry in case on my wedding day,
> I find my bride, my friend the Municipal Council.
> God may bless me with baby
> Claimed, though still in womb, by the Municipal Council.
> O, seller of radishes, one millim a bundle,
> How much for your kids and how much for the Municipal
>   Council?

The present sewage problem of Cairo has obviously a long history, well beyond the influx of the post 1967 war refugees, as we learn from Bayram:

> Our district is the jewel of the sewers,
> With a river flowing in its midst.
> Thanks to our Municipal Council
> Thanks to the flooding sewer
> We have now a swimming pool,
> Teaching nudity to our kids.
> And a vastly wide area,
> Teaches bridge-building to our elders.
> We have so many gulleys
> Long forgotten and ignored.
> In each one of these gulleys
> A ship mast may be sunk.
> In it a man may dive,

> Swallow, breath in and sneeze.
> Before he is finally drowned,
> They point to the steam pump!
> What is blinding us there,
> Are the flies swarming over the city.
> An engine, they said, is on its way
> In the workshop being repaired.
> Their energy is in full vigour,
> When an old hovel is in question,
> For it is a crime to pile bricks
> Attracting action from the inspector.
> O, cruel Municipal Council,
> Diligent in capturing seats.
> While we are waiting, they are made
>   into assets,
> And a proper commercial enterprise.

One day, Bayram read that there were four thousand advocates in Egypt, and the report drew from him this comment:

> In Egypt, there are four thousand lawyers,
> God protect me, said I, as I saw their number
> And as I discovered there are one million thieves,
> And each one, an entire case!

Bayram al-Tunisi lived on to see King Farouk sent to exile and the exiled poet returned to Egypt and celebrated with a long poem on the deposed king.

> Into palaces he strolls
> To lavish gifts on Narmim,
> And Auntie Cairo Radio
> Announces in every hour,
> The King is great in his qualities
> Generous in his bounties.

As Bayram al-Tunisi was famous in Egypt, Mullah Abbud al-Karkhi became famous in Iraq, but the similarity ends there. Bayram was a socialist, a progressive and a proletarian, whereas Mullah Abbud was a nationalist, a racist and a farmer. In style and subject matter, Bayram exhibited the gentleness and delicacy of the average Cairene whilst Mullah Abbud was the quintessence of the rugged

sharpness and the devil-take-all obscenities of the average Baghdadi.
With the total inability to convey in another language any measure
of this poet's obscene verses, one can only relate his story with King
Faisal I. The new King of Iraq was determined to win the good will of
his country's poets and writers by sponsoring them as members of
parliament. Somehow, Prime Minister Nuri al-Said failed to respond
to the king's pleasure in the case of Abbud al-Karkhi and the poet
went harking on about it and agitating that the colloquial poet was
no less an artist and noble thinker than those writing in classical
Arabic. The good king took note and went on urging his prime
minister to do justice to Abbud. What was wrong with his poetry, he
asked. Nuri al-Said was then forced into the unpleasant position of
giving his monarch a sample of it, but no sooner did he finish the
first line, than His Majesty put his hands on both ears, 'Enough!
Enough.' The king had asked for it and got it; my reader has not and I
have no right to invade his sensibilities by repeating to him what
the prime minister said to His Majesty.

With his agrarian background, Mullah Abbud al-Karkhi excelled
in using the rich language of the Middle-East peasantry and the oral
folklore of his country, especially parables and proverbs. During the
Anglo–Iraqi conflict over the Mandate and Britain's insistence on
'looking after' Iraq, al-Karkhi published a famous poem, 'The Wolf
and the Dog', in which he resorted to the old device of using an
animal story to illustrate a point. The dog saw the wolf hungry, tired
and desperate, and offered his advice. There was a place where he
could join the dog and have plenty of food and comfort. The wolf was
excited and followed the dog but half way he noticed the collar
round his neck. 'What is this, my dear doggy friend?' The dog told
him of its name and its purpose – to put him on a lead outside and
tether him inside. 'Oh, no, not for me,' said the wolf as he retraced his
steps,

> Not if you give me millions of camels, goats,
>   cows, sheep and gazelles!
> Never will I be chained or wear the ring
> Around my neck and accept humiliation! . . .
> Wolves we were born and fearless of foes
> Fearless of guns, swords and rifles.
> You, soft-minded dogs,
> You accept slavery and the control of women.

Iraq was conquered by the British Army and the British occupation and administration relied mainly on Indians in the lower echelons of office which had the direct contact and dealings with the population. The natives might have understood being pushed around by an Englishman, but not by an Indian, whom they considered beneath them. The racist connotations abound in Karkhi's pieces of bitter satire against these Indian occupiers.

> A short stocky Indian I saw,
> Like a shit on a mount,
> Like a shit mount on a hill,
> But with the sting of a scorpion.
> Take off your shoe and hit him,
> On his head, this shabby man.
> At Rumaitha I saw him sitting
> With the look of Satan and with his wicked soul.
> An heir to Abu Murra the devil
> From him he inherited his qualities.
> From Abu Murra he learnt
> All his tricks, this damned son.
> To the fox, he became a friend.
> Like him he had his eyes made up,
> Black, with teeth shining white,
> And eyes darting so.
> A nose, flat like a cow's dung,
> And hair curly all over.
> A horrid and most hated sight!

From this unbridled description, one cannot be sure whether the man was actually an Indian, but for Mullah Abbud, it sufficed that he was a member of the occupation forces. The immense popularity which his poetry achieved prompted him to enter the world of journalism by launching his satirical newspaper, *al-karkh*, which, like all similar publications, aroused the anger of the successive governments until the poet could find no lawyer willing to take the legal responsibility for it. Al-Karkhi was a typical Iraqi in his pessimism, dissatisfaction and continuous grumbling, now all made worse by this adventure into the world of journalism:

> With a needle we ate shit and shut our mouths.
> We gave up truth, just want to live.
> Honesty failed us and hurt us.
> It ruined us and made us penniless.

Brothers and neighbours disowned us.
Two-thirds of the nation are set against us
Who can tell the lion, 'your mouth stinks!'
And says it, though fearful and anxious.
Henceforth, I shall write fairy tales.
It is wiser and safer for my newspaper.
I shall write whatever they want,
About the roc, the si'lwa fairy and the demons,
About the bald-headed monster and the tantal.
Thus we'll be amused.
For if I spoke true and frank,
They will say this is libellous and defamatory.
Oh, the *Karkh*, what bitter poison it gave me
An ominous star it showed me in midday.

Not satisfied with the existing restrictions on the press, the
government promulgated a new Publications Law which put further
restraints on writers and reporters. Al-Karkhi responded with a
lament, 'The cat is gone, the mouse may play.' In another poem he
lamented the sad state of the Iraqi press and compared it with the
more favourable conditions in Syria, Lebanon and Egypt:

Whenever I try to socialize and be amicable
My words are never heeded.
In midstream, they tell me 'Don't kick up dust.'
They argued and proved I caused the sandstorm.
When I write about infamies,
'You are attacking people,' they say.
I don't know how to win my peace.
Is this my life and this my craft?
O, Arabs; my heart aches of the press,
My tears are flowing free on my cheeks.
May our press go as sacrifice,
For that of Egypt and its people.
Al-Kaukab and *al-Balagh* with their wonderful sense,
Al-Siyasa, Rose al-Youssef and *al-Kashkul*,
Criticizing their government and their Sa'ad Zaghlul
Creating crisis in Cairo all the time.
In Syria, there, *al-Dabbur*,
Lashes any traitor of the natives.
If we say one-tenth of what they say,
the Najaf cemetery will be our home, cursed by all.

The name of Ahmad Fu'ad Najm was mentioned in connection
with the June 1967 war with Israel and its aftermath. This
vernacular poet was influenced by Bayram al-Tunisi and like him,
was a socialist, only more of an indoctrinated revolutionary. He was
arrested many times by the security apparatus of President Sadat
and recorded in his poetry his experience with its agents. Ahmad
Fu'ad Najm has a deep-seated hatred for the Egyptian bourgeoisie
which flourished and reasserted itself under the open-door policies
of Sadat.

> You can see them
> At the centre of the town
> In motor cars like ships
> With bottoms like dough
> With stomachs all fat
> With skin shining white
> With brains so thick
> With teeth like files,
> Which cut the solid ice,
> No hot, no cold deters them.
> They eat the cast iron.
> So long as the river flows
> And comes from the Sa'id,
> Their revenue mounts
> And their stomachs increase.

In another poem he attacked the pampered 'educated class':

> Long live the intellectual in his feathered café
> Flamboyant and foppish
> Plenty of talk
> Absence of action
> Dislike of crowds
> With a few meaningless words
> A few definitions and terms
> He fabricates solutions
> For insoluble problems.
> Long live the intellectual!

Cairo Radio, which played such an important role in Arab politics,
was treated to a long poem:

> This is Shaqlaban
> The radio station, the sweetest in time,
> From Cairo and Kurduvan
> All Arab lands and Japan,
> Venezuela also and Iran,
> From any house or town,
> Raped by American tourism . . .
> We give you in all languages
> Drama, cinema and all literature,
> The press, oratory and television
> Speeches from mosques, cheese and olives,
> Plenty of rubbish, in all cases, at all times.
> No one listens and who cares.
> We are not bothered if you hear us or if you don't
> To eat *ex-gratia* is all that concerns us
> So hold your peace and do not cause us
> To unleash on you our pen and our tongue.

Ahmad Fu'ad Najm, like most Arabs, has always been excited by the visit of any guest and has shown his excitement in special poems as this one about President Nixon:

> We are honoured, O, Nixon.
> The man of Watergate.
> The sultans of olive oil and beans
> Hailed your value and status.
> For you they completed the widest road
> From Ras al-Tin to Mecca
> And from Mecca to Acre
> And said you made a holy pilgrimage.

In a similar poem, Najm welcomed Valery Giscard d'Estaing, the President of France, during his visit to Cairo:

> Valery Giscard d'Estaing,
> And also the lady his wife,
> They will grab the wolf by the tail
> And feed every hungry man.
> Oh, bless them, oh, lads,
> All those gentlemen.
> We shall soon be prosperous.
> Our life will be a heaven.

> Our television will be in colour.
> Many societies will be formed.
> The motor cars will run on perfume
> And will have no need for petrol.
> Great renaissance will rise
> In theatre, cinema and zoo.
> We only have to pay the price.
> All things will be like baklava.
> We shall not need Syria or Libya.
> We shall have our Arab unity
> With London and the Vatican.

Perhaps the most celebrated vernacular poet in the Arab World is now Muzaffar al-Nawab, a Marxist revolutionary who spent a few years in prison as a member of the Iraqi Communist Party. As a young teacher, he spent some fruitful years teaching peasant boys in South Iraq, where he learnt their dialect and absorbed their wonderful sense of poetry to give his nation an artist who may be compared favourably with the greatest pillars of Arabic literature. But for our purpose, he is inherently a romantic poet and humour comes to him in a humourless way with crude outbursts of obscenity and swearing, as evidenced in his poem which he recited at a mass meeting attended by ministers and top executives of the Syrian Government in the wake of the 1967 war, and in which he addressed himself to the rulers of the Arab World with these words, now quite famous: 'Ya awlad al-qahba' (O, sons of a whore).

It is more of a joy to hear Muzaffar al-Nawwab than to read him, and he is fortunate to live in the days of cassettes which provided us with many superb examples in this medium. Not many other vernacular poets were as fortunate as he is and the oral tradition of the genre and the dictatorial repression of the authorities deprived us of valuable treasures, and made the researcher's work more difficult.

More fortunate were the 'monologuists', who often wrote their own satirical and humorous verses in the vernacular, set them to their own music and sang them in cabarets or over the radio. Some achieved great success like Omar al-Zi'anni in Lebanon; a few made a considerable wealth like Mahmud Shukuku and Ismael Yasin in Egypt; and others spent a few spells in jail like Aziz Ali in Iraq. Soon after Nasser's revolution, Shukuku was arrested for singing a disgruntled song and the arrest warrant proved to be a signal from the soldiers to banish the art of the monologue from every part of the

Arab World. Arabic is a language which depends on the magic of its rhythm, rhymes, beat and mathematical symmetry. It was these qualities which gave poetry that grip on the Arabs. The modern poets have turned away from these values and opted for blank verse and free verse in imitation of English poetry and, like their counterparts in the West, they are gradually becoming isolated. Although most of them have written verses about the 1967 war, none of their poems achieved the widespread impact achieved by Ahmad Fu'ad Najm. With the obscurantism of their westernized and humourless poetry, pompous in spirit and thin in ideas, they may well be digging a grave for classical Arabic by making it even more remote from the uneducated majority. They may soon find that their place is taken over by the poetry of the vernacular with its lively wit and natural humour.

'The Developing World: Down with the Dollar!' Said Farmawi,
Al-Arab 1985.

Epilogue

> Laughter prevents the satisfaction of biological drives; it
> makes a man equally incapable of killing or copulating; it
> deflects anger, apprehension and pride.
>
> Sigmund Freud

From the preceding chapters, there emerges a rather bleak picture of
the Arab World, and the material presented in this book illustrates
that the Arabs are more aware than others of their unhappy state.
This is a healthy sign as awareness of the disease often helps the
wise patient in his fight for recovery and good health, which leads us
to the question whether the Arab is such a wise patient. Among
other things, the answer depends on how Arab leaders and thinkers
will treat the benign exposition of humour. Rulers of the Arab
peoples have often been terrified – and not without good justifi-
cation – of the emotionalism and explosive nature of their subjects.
As has been repeatedly argued in this work, humour does not appeal
to this side of man's character; it mainly deals with his intellect and
power of reason, and it does that in a cool and dispassionate manner.
No one can kill and laugh at the same time, a fact which is
demonstrated by the substantial space given in this book to Egypt
and the Egyptians.

Writers, artists and journalists have often been invited to
criticize, discuss and expose, but in a cool manner free from
provocation, agitation and emotional rabble-rousing. If this kind of
harmless criticism is to be given an artistic frame with a general
appeal, then humour is one of the most suitable channels, which
will also give the necessary vent for all the socio-political pressures
and frustrations, and signal a new spirit of self-confidence and
maturity.

The disenchantment of the Arab peoples with their political
regimes embodied in their satirical indictments should not cloud
the true picture and transform it into an irredeemable conglo-

meration of black shadows. This is a picture which is part of the bleak panorama of the whole Third World, and as such it stands out as one of its few brighter spots. Even in the darkest days of contemporary oppression, no Arab country has gone through what has been happening in many parts of Africa, Latin America, the Far East and even Europe under the heels of the Fascists and the Stalinists. No mass graves of hundreds of liquidated opponents have been uncovered in the Arab World as they were in Central and Eastern Europe, Cambodia and Argentina. No one has died of famine in the independent Arab countries and no serious epidemic has swept through their towns and villages. With all their warfare and violent outrages, the Arabs have generally shown more respect to the centres of learning, mosques, churches, synagogues and historical sites than was shown by the Germans, the British and the Americans in the Second World War. Arab political and military defeats shrink to minor reverses when put into the perspective of the endless designs and ambitions of the powerful Zionist Movement, its American backers and practically all the foreign powers against the emergent nations of the Middle East.

The incessant Arab grumbling is a sign of maturity, experience and awareness of one's rights and national expectations. The widespread pessimism and cynicism are partly due to the two factors of time and place. With such glorious civilizations and military achievements behind them, the Arabs cannot stop brooding over the comparison between their present and their past. That history was constantly bedevilled with the conflict with Europe, which made them look all the time over their shoulder to the north, check and compare. From the earliest days of their new *nahdha* (awakening) they identified themselves psychologically with Europe, wearing European clothes, borrowing European musical instruments, dancing the waltz and the tango, and even speaking French at home. Typical is the way they looked down at other Asians and Africans.

All this may be harmless and quaint, but the comedy became a tragedy when the imitation failed in the political field. Only a few days are needed to learn dancing or driving a motor car, but one needs years of psychological accumulation to appreciate the democracy developed by Europe over many centuries.

To aspire to the achievment of the highest is a sign of man's greatness and, alas, the cause of his sadness. The Arabs will undoubtedly go on striving and, in this long and frustrating struggle, their old sense of humour should recommend itself as the best, the cheapest and safest palliative.

Notes

Introduction
1. Bergson, H., *Laughter*, London 1913, pp. 43, 48.
2. Koestler, A., *The Act of Creation*, London 1969, p. 51.
3. Aqqad, A., *Mutala'at fi al-Kutub*, Beirut 1966, p. 132.
4. Rosenthal, F., *Humour in Early Islam*, Connecticut 1976, pp. 136-7.
5. Aristotle, *Poetics*, Cambridge University Press 1960.
6. Bergson, op.cit., pp. 16-17.
7. Freud, S., *Jokes and Their Relations to the Unconscious*, London 1960, p. 103.

Chapter 1: The Zarif and His Art
1. Arabism (*uruba*) has become identified in modern times with Arab nationalism. In earlier periods, it signifies a form of tribal allegiance to the Arab race.
2. Meredith, G.,*The Idea of Comedy*, London 1906, pp. 59-60.
3. *Nihayat al-Arab*, 4-4.
4. Aqqad, A.M., *Juha, The Laughing Comedian*, Cairo.
5. Rosenthal, F., *Humour in Early Islam*, Connecticut 1976, p. 30.
6. Abu al-Tayib al-Washa', *al-Zarf wa al-Zurafa'*, 1906.
7. *Qur'an*, 5-45-49.
8. Cited in Abd al-Majid, A., *Rihla Ma'a al-Zurafa'*, Cairo.
9. Citation in Rosenthal, op.cit., p. 133.

Chapter 2: Political Humour in Arab History
1. Al-Tawhidi, *Al-Imta' wa al-Mu'anasa*, Vol. III, p. 175.
2. Al-Qayrawani, *Zahr al-Adab*, Vol.III, p. 771-3.
3. Al-Tawhidi, *Al-Imta' wa al-Mu'anasa*, Vol. III, p. 184.
4. *Ilam-en-Nas*, translation by G. Clerk, London 1873, p. 74.
5. Ibn al-Muqaffa', *Kalila wa Dimna*, translated by Ramsay Wood, Granada, London 1982, p. 47.
6. Rich Muslims of the Middle Ages used to castrate male slaves to employ them in the service of the harem. The operation deprived

them of their beards and other apparent features of men.
7. To Medieval Arabs, black referred to the sons of the Negro race. All other races were white.
8. c.f. Rajab al-Najjar, M., *Juha the Arab*, Kuwait.

Chapter 3: The Age of Resurgence: the Satirical Press
1. Abduh, I., *Abu Naddara*, Cairo 1953, p. 20.
2. The published report cites 'kidneys' but this must be an editorial gloss contradicting Arabic idiom and physiological facts! Arabs do not make mistakes in such matters on the whole.
3. For accounts of Sannu's life, see Irene L. Gendzier, *The Practical Visions of Ya'qub Sannu*, Harvard University Press 1966.
4. The foregoing extracts and other samples of al-Nadim's writings are given in *Sulafat al-Nadim fi Muntakhabat al-Sayid Abdullah al-Nadim*, Cairo 1914.
5. c.f. Hamza, A., *The Art of Journalistic Articles in Egypt*, Vol. III, Cairo.
6. The Arabic equivalent to Tom, Dick and Harry.
7. We are indebted for much of the foregoing citations to Ibrahim Abduh, *Rose al-Youssef*, Cairo.
8. Al-Jundi, Anwar, *The Political Press*, Cairo 1962, p. 347.
9. Eminent Egyptian scholar, author and leader of the Constitutional Liberal Party during the monarchy.
10. *Kawakab al-Sharq*, 4 June 1933.
11. Al-Alusi, J., *Taha Hussein*, Baghdad 1973, p. 206.
12. Accounts of his writings are to be found in Batti, Raphael, *Al-Sahafa fi al-Iraq*, Baghdad 1955.
13. Zubaidi, A., *Arabic Drama in Iraq*, The Institute of Arab Research and Studies, Baghdad 1966, pp. 118 and 126.

Chapter 4: The Age of Resurgence: the Men of Wit
1. Amin, M., *Min Wahid li 'Ashra*, Cairo 1977, p. 200.
2. Ibid., p. 142.
3. Haykal, M. Husein, *Muthakkirat*, Cairo 1951, Vol.I, p. 169.
4. Translation from Arabic of al-Aqqad's biography, *Sa'ad Zaghlul*.
5. More episodes are given by his biographers, Hanna Khabbaz and George Haddad in *Faris al-Khuri*, Beirut 1952.
6. Amin, M., *Sana al-Si jn*, Cairo 1978, pp. 169-71.
7. Amin, M., *Sana Rabi'a Si jn*, Cairo 1981, pp. 171-6.
8. Haykal, M. Husein, op. cit., p. 23.
9. Abu Isa, Fathi, *Al-Fukaha fi al-Adab al-Arabi*, Algiers 1970, pp. 271-2.

10. Al-Hufi, Ahmad Muhamad, *Al-Fukaha fi al-Adab*, Cairo 1966, pp. 139-40.

Chapter 5: The Age of the Cynic
1. Abduh, I. *Rasa'il min Nifaqistan*, Cairo 1974, pp. 84-7.
2. Malik, A., *Ayyam Lubnaniya wa Arabiya*, Beirut 1968, p. 107.
3. Ibid., p. 62.
4. *Al-Ahram*, 17 September 1934.

Chapter 6: The Golden Age of Nasser
1. Abduh, I., *Rasa'il min Nifaqistan*, Cairo 1974, p. 49.
2. Abu Zaid, Ahmad, *Alam al-Fikr*, October 1983, p. 715.
3. Bergson, op. cit., p. 4.
4. Amin, M., *Sana Rabi'a Si jin*, Cairo 1981, p. 50.
5. Siba'i, Y., *Ayyam ma'a Abd al-Nasser*, Cairo 1971, p. 9.
6. Nutting, A., *Nasser*, London 1972, p. 72.
7. Siba'i, Y., op.cit., p. 19.
8. Abduh, I., 1974, op.cit., p. 112.

Chapter 7: The Trauma of the Naksa
1. *Attadamon*, 9 June 1984.

Chapter 8: The Rifle and the Pen
1. Cited from the BBC Monitoring Report, ME 7074/A/4.
2. A reference to the famous Iraqi poet, al-Jawahiri, who sided with the communists against the nationalists.

Chapter 9: The Vernacular Poets
1. Al-Jahiz, *Al-Bayan wa al-Tabiyin*, Vol. I, p. 145.
2. Hamza, Abd al-Latif, *Adab al-Maqala al-Sahafia fi Misr*, Vol., I, p. 29.
3. Ibid., p. 43.